ROGER PULVERS is an author, playwright, theater director, translator and filmmaker. He has published more than fifty books in Japanese and English, including novels, essays, plays, and poetry. Working as assistant to director Oshima Nagisa on *Merry Christmas, Mr. Lawrence* brought him back to Japan and inspired him to become the award-winning playwright, film director and prolific author he is today. His novel, *Hoshizuna Monogatari (Star Sand)*, which he wrote in Japanese, was published by Kodansha, Japan's largest publisher, in 2015, and subsequently in English and French in 2016 and 2017 respectively. It was released as a film, directed by him, in 2017. His most recent books are the novels, *Half of Each Other* and *Peaceful Circumstances*, his autobiography, *The Unmaking of an American*, and a cultural memoir, *My Japan*, all published by Balestier Press.

Preface

For many years I resisted translating Takuboku's tanka. The reason was that I could not see a way of doing it with a feeling of accomplishment. The primary criterion for a good translation is that the translated work reads well. The reader of the translated work should be moved in a similar way as the reader of the original, experiencing the same depths of emotion.

Then I began to realize that Takuboku's tanka have a very concrete message in them. They are masterful because they are so crystal clear, like perfectly cut little diamonds. Needless to say, this does not mean that they are not often vague, ambiguous and beautifully suggestive. They are packed with nuanced connotations of a linguistic and emotive nature.

Any translation would have to capture these two seemingly contradictory qualities: concreteness and suggestiveness. I had always been unmoved by the kinds of translations of haiku and tanka that seemed, for lack of a better term, "pseudo-Oriental." The wispy and puffy nature of the language used in the translation, often without personal pronouns or verb, left the poems hanging in the air. This quality presumed to capture the symbolic redolence of the original.

But to me this was a misreading of the original qualities. Yes, the originals are evocative and redolent. But these very qualities must be clearly stated in a translation for them to evoke those effects. This may sound paradoxical, that you need to be very clear and concrete in order to be vague and suggestive. To me this became evident. The reverberations enter the mind and heart after the poem is taken in. Let the light radiate in all its beauty and subtlety after it leaves the perfect surfaces of the cut diamond.

Now, each genre of translation presents a different variety of challenge and demands a separate kind of talent.

Translating a short story or a novel is the easiest. You ask yourself what the author is trying to say and how they are trying to say it. You create a voice for the author/narrator of the story and speak with it in your own language.

Translating a play is not so easy. The characters have a life of their own—what might be called a "verbal personality"—and this has to be expressed in many different voices. It is not enough "to become" the playwright. You need to be able to faithfully reproduce the speech patterns and quirky logic used by any number of people. You need to create many authentic voices.

Translating poetry is the hardest of all. The poems have to work in your own language as poems. If they don't, no matter how "faithful" you are to the language of the original, no matter how textually correct you are, the result will be unsatisfactory. Readers will naturally react by saying, "I'm sorry, but I just don't see why the work of this poet is valued so highly in their own country." You have to recreate not only the language, voice and personality of the poet but also the mood, nuances and suggestiveness of the poems. Among poetry translation, the rendering of haiku and tanka into another language presents the greatest difficulty. It is like climbing a mountain covered in dangerous crevices, roads to nowhere and sharp cliffs. I have found this the case, as well, in the fifty years I have spent translating the poetry of Miyazawa Kenji, whose many scientific and Buddhist references, not to mention puzzling non sequiturs, make the task difficult enough. Now, with Takuboku, the crevices seem even deeper, the roads to nowhere more frequently encountered and the cliffs high enough to strain your neck just looking up at them. That is why I avoided climbing Mt. Takuboku. Suggestiveness, multiple reverberating meanings, ambivalence, extreme lyricism and unashamed sentimentality, the brevity of the genre … and all done in a package that has a concrete and impactful poetic message. I didn't consider myself up to the task. How would it be possible to render this all into English and come out with a poem at the end that leaves a strong impression on the reader?

Translation of poetry is similar to directing in the theater. You need to have a stark and clear vision of the whole—in the case of poetry, the poem; in the case of theater, the play—in order to achieve an artistic effect. You cannot just have the actors speak the dialogue and assume that the audience will glean meaning and dramatic impact from the words. You cannot just translate the words of a poem literally and correctly and assume that the reader will be moved. You need to ask yourself in the case of poetry, "What is this poem trying to say? What effects on the emotions and the intellect is the poet aiming for?" In order to translate a poem, you need to interpret its words in a context that will make perfect sense to the person who reads it in a foreign language.

I have chosen, in this collection, to give titles to the tanka, even though there are no titles in the original poems. This is one way to give focus and concrete intent to them. It is also a sneaky way of adding information, meaning and, in some cases, nuance while keeping the translations short at three lines.

Though he died well over a century ago, Takuboku is in many ways our contemporary. He is in touch with his subconscious mind in a way that resonates with us. Modern psychology and psychiatry have opened up new worlds of understanding of human nature. Takuboku anticipates many aspects of this understanding. He is brutally frank about the relationships he is in with family and friends, as objective about his own foibles as he is about those of others. He is socially and politically committed; and he is self-deprecating about his inability or reluctance to take action. Had he been writing in a language like English or French or German or any other frequently translated European language, I am convinced he would have had an immense influence on world literature. As it is, he has had that influence on Japanese literature and on the culture of the Japanese people.

Perhaps now Takuboku's poetic genius will be known a little bit more to those outside Japan.

It is a coincidence, perhaps, that Japan's two greatest modern poets, Ishikawa Takuboku and Miyazawa Kenji, were born about fifty kilometers from each other, were only ten years apart in age and went to the same middle school. Both also died young from tuberculosis, Takuboku at twenty-six; and Kenji, at thirty-seven.

But Takuboku achieved much greater fame than Kenji in the twentieth century. Even in their native Iwate, children studied and memorized Takuboku's tanka for decades, while Kenji was thought of as somehow being non-mainstream, not "representative" of Japanese culture. Today both poets are celebrated equally throughout Japan.

Kenji was a supernova that exploded in 1933: The light is just beginning to reach us now. Takuboku has always been a shower of shooting stars, the kind of shower that comes back year after year and never ceases to dazzle and delight us.

It is my fervent wish that the light from the poetry of these two poets will reach people all over the world for many years to come.

Roger Pulvers
2020

PART ONE

Love Family Friends

We look back today at the Meiji era (1868-1912) and think of it as stodgy, old fashioned and in many ways retrogressive in social attitudes. But this is very much a view with the bias of hindsight. Actually, Meiji Japan was a dynamic and progressive era full of activism, agitation and genuinely democratic energy.

In many ways Japan then was like a western European country. The culture, thanks to what is called *bunmei kaika* (the adoption of "civilization and enlightenment" from the West), flourished in unplanned and cosmopolitan ways. Not only intellectuals but people from various walks of life and layers of society knew the works of Swedish playwright August Strindberg; they read Russian literature avidly; they quoted French poetry in Japanese; they admired English values and manners; they immersed themselves in German science and philosophy ... all these became part of the social discourse of the nation.

Yet despite the huge amount of cultural borrowing that *bunmei kaika* introduced, there was a healthy pride in the native culture of Japan. And though the social elites of the society strove to protect their privilege and wealth, there was a lively discourse on social and cultural issues carried out by progressive intellectuals, many of them, such as authors Natsume Soseki, Mori Ogai and Nagai Kafu, and scientist Minakata Kumagusu, who had extensive exposure to European and American life.

But while the society and the economy seemed to progress, what was happening inside the Meiji family and how did this affect the life of Ishikawa Takuboku?

The key to the answer to this is found in the role of women in the family and society.

As we look back from our feminist perspective of the twenty-first century, it is easy to criticize Meiji Japan for its horrid treatment of women. We all know that women had to walk "three steps" behind their husband. In fact, the life of a woman could be characterized as being under the foot of her father as a girl, under the thumb of her husband (and his mother) as a woman, and under the strict "guidance" of her son as a mother. Only late in life, when mother-in-law and husband were dead, and son was no longer at home, could she be herself, which accounts for why many old ladies in Japan seemed to be so happy.

Actually, however, the situation for Japanese women in Meiji Japan, as bad as it was, was not so different from that for women in the West. Japanese women did not get the right to vote until 1945; but French women could not vote until 1944, and Italian women until 1946. Women were socially oppressed everywhere, not just in Japan.

And the very notion of the "ideal woman" in the Meiji era came largely from Victorian England, not basically from aspects of traditional Japanese society. Women in Victorian England and Meiji Japan who worked were generally scorned; and if something happened to their children, even illness caused by bacteria or viruses well beyond their control, they were blamed for neglect, and they often blamed themselves as well. Motherhood was seen as the sole aspiration of a woman's emotional and practical needs. The man was the head of the household, the moral patriarch. The woman was required to serve, honor and obey him. That was the very definition of female "love." A woman who refused to take part in this covenant was seen either as fated to have a miserable and lonely existence as a spinster or as an immoral and "loose" woman. The woman's sole "creative" role was in the upbringing of her sons. I say creative, but such creativity was just an act of proactive self-sacrifice.

"The hand that rocks the cradle rules the world" is a proverb of Victorian England, and by "the world" the Victorians meant "the British empire." In other words, a woman's role in life was to produce young men who would go out and fight for empire and give up their life, if necessary, for "king and country." This is precisely the model that Japan adopted and followed, taking patriotism to a Japanese extreme of loyal devotion in the first two decades of the Showa era (1926-1989).

The popular phrase that illustrated the picture of the "ideal woman" in Meiji Japan was *ryosai kenbo*, which meant "a good wife and a clever mother." Now we view this as regressive and oppressive; but in the Meiji era it was a very progressive idea created by one of the towering figures of the time, Nakamura Masanao.

Nakamura Masanao was a scholar, translator, educator and philanthropist. He spent two years in Britain, returning to Japan a few months after the emperor was restored to the throne in 1868. He translated, among other works, John Stuart Mill's *On Liberty*. Even today, a quote from this inspires us, just as it would have inspired people in Takuboku's day ...

The only purpose for which power can be rightfully exercised over any member of a civilized community, against his will, is to prevent harm to others. His own good, either physical or moral, is not a sufficient warrant . . . Over himself, over his body and mind, the individual is sovereign.

These were the kinds of ideas propagated by Nakamura Masanao in Japan and deeply felt by people like Ishikawa Takuboku; and they fired up two generations of men to create a relatively just Japanese society. That a woman was supposed to be a good wife and clever mother was seen as an important element in creating the kind of society where men could flourish and prosper. Women at the time did not enjoy the kind of personal freedom that men did in any country of the world. If they protected the home, they were considered a vital link in society's strong chain. If they opted out of the role of good wife and clever mother, they were frowned upon and scorned. Many traditional societies in the developing world today have exactly this view of women. Of course, this is in no way whatsoever right or just; and it can never be justified with pseudo-religious or cultural excuses. But at the time in Japan and in the nations of the European imperial powers such "service" was seen as not only right and just but necessary for the creation of a powerful nation state.

We may look upon Takuboku's open infidelity (many more words than acts), his emotional neglect of his wife and daughter, and his male selfishness with some disdain. But in being this way he was no different from millions upon millions of men in all other countries at the time. This, of course, may explain such behavior, but it does not excuse it.

Takuboku was highly conflicted with inner torment about his relationship with his wife, daughter and mother. And he had a major problem with friends too. He said in his *Diary in Roman Letters*, a diary he wrote not in a Japanese script but in Roman letters, that all friendship is superficial. Perhaps he was unable to fully trust himself, and this prevented him from fully trusting others.

What Takuboku does offer us, however—and this makes his writing so very meaningful for us today—is honest and profound self-examination, heartfelt confessions of guilt, and the passionate aspiration to be a better husband and a better father. He is racked by self-pity, and this self-pity often feeds his self-centered view of his relationships.

But is he any different from poets and authors in later eras in Japan?

There are so many such male dominators who bewail their selfish behavior toward women and their family members but do nothing whatsoever to change their behavior that I won't list their names here because such a list would take up too many paragraphs. At least Takuboku knows that he is not behaving as he should toward his wife and daughter, and he tries to make amends. He is very sensitive to how others view him, too, and wants to *appear* to be a good husband and a clever father. Some of the tanka in this chapter illustrate that aspiration very clearly.

One of the reasons why we value his tanka so highly today is that we recognize his honesty and openness as genuine. As with an actor so it is with a poet: An insincere "performance" may fool many people for some time if it appears to be truthful. But in the long run, audiences and readers see through insincerity and recognize it for what it is: a bluff for a lack of candor. Takuboku is not bluffing. He puts every aspect of his character on the line for us to judge.

It is easy for us to be holier-than-thou when it comes to comparisons of our behavior with that of people of a previous day.

Yet, we are guilty of very similar oppressive actions today. By comparing ourselves favorably with people of the past, we may simply be trying to justify how progressive we ourselves are, thereby masking our own reactionary behavior.

Japan today craves writers who have the integrity of self-expression and the clarity of vision on their society that Takuboku expresses to us. In the mirror of his works, we are compelled to see our own face in a clear and honest light.

SURPRISE

My daughter's face lit up
When I yanked the cat's ear
And it yelped "Meow!"

Yank, yelp and meow are mimetic words, as are *nyato* (meow) and *bikkuri* (surprise) in the original.

ON A LARK

I lifted my mother onto my back.
She was so light I wept
Stopped dead after three steps.

"Stopped dead" is used here because the word "dead" suggests that his mother is not long for this world. "On a lark" is an equivalent of *tawamureni*, which can also be conveyed with "just for fun." This is one of Takuboku's most well-known and often quoted tanka.

IN MY DARKENED ROOM

I turned off the oil lamp, alone
As my father and my mother walked out of the wall
Each holding a cane.

This is one of those images in which what is reality for the person experiencing it may seem like something surreal to the person reading about it. It also suggests a disarray in Takuboku's mind.

INTIMACY

When I compare myself unfavorably with my friends
I buy a bouquet for my wife
To cherish her.

This famous tanka, taught to children in Japanese schools, is a difficult one to translate because Takuboku merely suggests what will transpire between himself and his wife with the word *shitashimu* (to become familiar or intimate with). I settled on the English word "cherish." It has a number of nuances, from wishing to protect someone to loving them. The title, "Intimacy," adds to the suggestiveness of what Takuboku and Setsuko may do now that he is home and striving to make up for what he sees as his inadequacies.

LOVE

I want to try to love like a man
Burying his burning cheek
In soft drifts of snow.

The words that Takuboku uses to describe the snow have a lyrical beauty and sonority in Japanese—*yawarakani tsumoreru yuki ni*. I have tried to produce a similarly lyrical effect with "in soft drifts of snow."

WEATHER

The rain brings out the worst
In every single member of my family.
Oh for one clear day!

When I read this translation to my wife, who was born in Britain, she laughed and exclaimed, "That's just like a British family!" Japan and Britain seem to have more in common than just a lot of rain.

THE BUNDLE

It weighs on me that I can't remember where
I put the bundle of love letters from my wife
Eight years ago now.

The contrast of "eight years ago" and "now" seems crucial to me in this tanka. Unlike the photographs of the woman in MOVING HOUSE (see page fifty-two), these letters are neatly in a bundle. The problem is, where are they now?

MEMORIES

I started to take off my glove but stopped
When memories of her touch
Stole into my heart.

Takuboku is a man often plagued by his memories. They return to him when he is awake as well as when he is dreaming. They are a source of his intense sorrow and his creativity at the same time. This is brought out even more keenly in the next tanka.

MEMORY

Dozing on my belly on a sand dune
Brings back every single distant pain
Of first love.

This painful and all-too-present memory is characterized by the contrasting usage of the word *toi*, or distant. A memory may be far away in time or place and yet be real and alive within us right here and now. There is an erotic nuance in this tanka. He is on top of something soft and pliable, the sand. It is this sensation that triggers the memories of love.

ONE DAY

I waited for her hour upon hour
Yet she never showed up. So, I carried
My little writing table to where it is now.

This tanka should appeal to anyone who writes. Has Takuboku given up on her? Or is he moving his writing table so that he can get down to work and forget her ... or because he will be able to write her a letter "from another angle"?

TABULA RASA

My little daughter insisted
That you couldn't write words on unlined paper.
To be so innocent!

I used the Latin (and also English) phrase "tabula rasa" for the title, to describe both the mind of his young daughter and a blank sheet of paper. Takuboku often seems to envy children their innocence, which he actually has not lost. In this way he resembles Kenji. Both of them retain their child's eye on the world, though Takuboku's gaze is much more "impure" than Kenji's.

BIRTH

That postcard about the birth
Put a smile on my lips
That would not go away.

There are quite a few postcards written by Takuboku in the Ishikawa Takuboku Memorial Museum at Shibutami in Iwate. Letters in the Meiji era were rather formal. The postcard was suited to penning a quick message, like today's Twitter. I changed the reference in the last line from that of a face to that of the lips in a smile. The literal translation of the original *kao o hareyaka ni shiteita* is "brightened up my face," a phrase that comes across as stilted and awkward in English.

WHEN WAS IT NOW?

I felt the joy of her voice
Flash in a dream
Her voice long gone from me now.

In the original the verb "to hear" *(kiku)* is repeated. In English I felt that the best word to repeat was, somehow, "voice."

FIVE YEARS AGO

Those old letters!
How could I have been so close
To a man like that?

Takuboku often refers to things in the past that happened four, five or eight years earlier. Here it is five years, not so long ago for most people. When we read these tanka now, they remind us poignantly of how short his life was, a mere twenty-six years. To a person of such a young age—and one who has tuberculosis and may not live long—"five years ago" can already be "far in the past." Even such a short time produces long-lasting regrets.

SORROW

Why do I feel sorrow as my daughter
Grows taller and stronger
Day by day?

This tanka is a question that Takuboku is posing to himself. Yet he well knows the answer: that time is running out for him and he may never see his little daughter Kyoko grow into adulthood. As it turned out, he died before her sixth birthday.

THE STARE

I sat my daughter at my bedside
And gave her a cold stare that sent her
Rushing out of the room.

Takuboku is well aware of the effect he can have on his child. Having been ill for so long, he must look rather frightening in the eyes of a little girl. Perhaps she wasn't used to spending time with him as well, as he was away from home for such long periods. The Japanese word used for "cold hard stare" is *majimajito*, which has the connotation of a sustained seriousness.

GROWING UP

I thought her a pain
From the time of her birth.
And now she is turning five.

Again, as in the previous tanka, regret for having been an absent father. I sense here the hope that if and when he recovers from his illness (if he ever does), he will try to dedicate more time to his daughter. Who, one wonders, is the person "growing up"?

MY DAUGHTER

It grieves me to think that she will not cry
When scolded or spanked
For I was like that too.

All of us who are parents often recall ourselves as children when we observe our own children, as Takuboku is, with some regret, doing here.

TO MY WIFE

Is it my thoughts that you are after
As I fix my eyes
On a single spot on the tatami?

Again, an intimate domestic scene and a link between Takuboku's inner and outer selves. Is there a poet who is as good as Takuboku at describing the silent moments in our lives? The tiny room that Takuboku and Setsuko spent their married days in is envisioned here. Their home in Morioka, that they shared with his parents, his younger sister and another family, is open to the public. You can see their room today.

WORDS

My daughter is picking up words like
"Workers" and "Revolution"
At the tender age of five.

The vocabulary of children is very much affected by the kinds of words they hear at home. She picks up these words but hardly understands them. But then again, did the adults of the era in Japan really understand the implications of the words "workers" and "revolution"? Takuboku may have considered himself a socialist, but he was a man of words, not action.

MY DAUGHTER

What's got into her?
She tossed her toys aside and came to sit beside me
Quietly, submissively.

Takuboku uses the adverb *otonashiku* to express the way his daughter comes to sit beside him. This is a Japanese word with many nuances: "without sound," "still," "in a well-behaved manner." It is often best, then, to use more than one word in such cases. I chose two that I thought appropriate for the relationship between this father and his daughter, and the sense of surprise he felt at her actions.

HAVING FUN

While my daughter is out with friends
I pull out the train set locomotive
And make it run.

Here Takuboku reminds me of Giovanni, the boy who is the main character in Kenji's *Night on the Milky Way Train*. There is an innocence expressed in many of Takuboku's tanka, an innocence that nearly always ensconces loneliness. In addition, Takuboku, like many men of his era, longed to have a son. (His wife did give birth to a son who died not long after birth.) In his day, a train set was essentially a toy for boys. Did his daughter sense that this toy may not have been for her?

BEDDING

I want to weep but walk out instead
To lose myself in the caresses
Of the inn's soft bedding.

Like another Tohoku writer who was born about three years before Takuboku died, Dazai Osamu also escaped from the trials of family life to take refuge in caresses. Dazai is much more explicit, however, about the kinds of caresses he goes after. Takuboku prefers to use the euphemism of the bedding (*yagu*). Takuboku writes much about other women, and he did fall in love with two or three of them. But it is unknown today how far these relationships went. Perhaps he wants to escape to the inn's soft bedding just to get away from the noises and hardships of his family life.

A FRIEND

I opened myself up to him
And felt I had lost something
Before we parted.

Takuboku often writes about his friends and the complex relationship he had with them. There is not only affection in these relationships: There is pity, envy and remorse.

MY FRIEND

His grumbling is deep
But his talent shallow.
And my pity for him knows no bounds.

No doubt his friend here feels that his great talent is going unrecognized, and so
he grumbles in complaint. Takuboku feels sorry for his friend ... or does he simply
find him pitiable?

MY DROLL FRIEND

The blue fatigue that was on the face
Of my droll dead friend
Has stayed with me.

Here there is no irony about or disdain for an old friend, merely a sense of loss that
will not go away.

WELL, WELL

Well, well
So *he* fathered a child!
I think I'll sleep soundly tonight.

This is a reference to his best friend Kindaichi Kyosuke becoming a father. Poet and scholar Kindaichi, who helped Takuboku out of many a problematic situation, was rather stitched up compared to Takuboku, who wore his heart perpetually on his sleeve. This tanka expresses a real fondness for a friend, while being at the same time an incisive comment on that friend's personality. Kindaichi survived Takuboku by nearly sixty years.

THE OLD ME

It's been years since I unsettled my parents
By announcing that I was
Going to join the army.

Takuboku, like the vast majority of Japanese at the time, was filled with patriotic pride for the military and its victories. Did he change his mind about the direction that his country was going in during the last few years of his life? Or is he just showing compassion for his parents, who might have worried that they could have lost a son, had he joined the army.

FOR SOME REASON

For some reason or other
It pleases me to call my five-year-old daughter
By the Russian name Sonya.

I think, actually, that Takuboku has a very good idea of why he is pleased to call his daughter Sonya. Sonya is a main character in Dostoevsky's novel *Crime and Punishment*. She is a prostitute but a woman of pure character and Christian virtue. Sonya is also the Russian nickname of Sophia, the goddess of wisdom. It is also possible that this Sonya represents a character in a book by the Russian revolutionary thinker and author, Pyotr Kropotkin. Takuboku was an ardent fan of his work.

CAUGHT IN THE MIDDLE

I seethe alone in sorrow
With no way to put an end to this discord
And estrangement.

Takuboku is caught in the middle of a number of relationships: those involving himself, his wife, his daughter and his parents, not to mention those with his friends and colleagues. The reference here is, in all probability, specifically to the relationship between his wife and his mother, in which he is "caught." At any rate, his helplessness is evident here. All he can do to assuage his anger is write about it.

CAT

Why bring a cat into my miserable home?
Even a cat would sow a seed
Of discord.

Even a cat would be "caught in the middle" in the Ishikawa household. The novelist Natsume Soseki first published, in serial form, his droll novel *I am a Cat* in the magazine "Hototogisu," beginning in January 1905, several years before Takuboku wrote this tanka. But Takuboku didn't have the detachment to be so whimsical about a cat in his house as Soseki did. Incidentally, Soseki attended Takuboku's funeral.

ONE DAY

I mooed like a cow
Suddenly forgetting how sick I was.
My wife and daughter are nowhere to be seen.

There is a witty absurdity in some of Takuboku's tanka, and this one has just that; although the fact that he is alone and ill underscores his isolation. Is it a coincidence that his wife and daughter are not there? Or are they not there because they cannot stand to be with him when he is mooing like a cow? He knows himself better than anyone.

ANTS

My sad sad father!
Yet another day sees him tossing aside his newspaper
And amusing himself with the tiny ants in the garden.

"Like father, like son" is an English saying that Takuboku might not have liked. After all, his father was a Buddhist priest, a far cry from being the dissolute writer and sometime agitator he was. But I cannot help but feel that this description of his father is just as clearly a description of himself. One of Takuboku's most famous tanka has him amusing himself with a crab (see page 120).

TEA

My mother went so far
As to give up tea to pray for my recovery.
So, what's she cross about again today?

Is his mother cross because she had given up tea or because her son has not recovered from his illness? He writes that she is cross about *nanika* (something or other). He can't fathom her thoughts or actions. Be that as it may, this encounter between mother and son is not a happy one.

BEFORE WE WERE MARRIED

My wife once longed
To have a life in music.
Now she sings no longer.

Setsuko, it seems, is no longer a happy person. And married life, especially in Takuboku's era, saw women having almost no chance to possess any time for themselves. Every waking moment was taken up with caring for husband, children and in-laws. Takuboku is certainly showing sympathy for her. But there is nothing he can—or is willing enough—to do about it.

JESUS

It grieved me that my little sister
Looked upon me with such pity
When I said, "Jesus was just a man."

Arguments about religion or politics can divide a family. But was Takuboku trying to provoke his little sister or engender pity for himself on purpose? His sister, Mitsuko, had attended a mission school in Nagoya, Seishi Jogakuin. With its deliberate barb as social commentary, this is a poem that feels very contemporary with issues in Western society today.

TO MY DAUGHTER

Don't take after your father
Or your father's father.
That's what your father hopes for you.

The word *oya* (parent or, here, father) appears three times in this tanka, underscoring the obsessiveness over family relationships in them. His parents may know him better than anyone ... which is precisely what is expressed in the next tanka.

IN A DREAM

My mother came to me in a dream
And with tears in her eyes said
"Oh, I see right through you now."

Carl Jung, the Swiss psychoanalyst, was just developing his ideas about the subconscious, introversion and extroversion around the time of Takuboku's death. In fact, he published his ground-breaking book, *Psychology of the Unconscious* in 1912, the year of Takuboku's death. Both Jung and Freud, though entertaining very different methods, knew about the importance of dreams to a person's psyche and personality. I wonder how they would have interpreted Takuboku's dreams, had he been psychoanalyzed by them.

dragging their family along, in search of work. The Meiji Restoration of 1868 saw great waves of upheaval in all aspects of social life, and people were carried on those waves. Big cities such as Tokyo and Osaka were the usual repositories for these waves of "internal migrants"; but many, especially people from Tohoku, went to distant places such as Hokkaido, which was to Japan what the West was once to America, a place of opportunity where the indigenous population had been all but wiped out or displaced. Land and opportunity seemed waiting to be taken. In his poem from the early 1920s titled "Asahikawa," which is a small town in Hokkaido, Kenji refers to the horse cart he is riding on through the town "in the colonial style." Is it really the town itself and not the carriage that he sees as being a kind of far-flung Japanese colony at the time? Hokkaido was, in a sense, a newly-settled colony of Japan proper at the time … and Takuboku was there fifteen years before Kenji wrote that poem.

Mobility created the kind of atmosphere in Meiji Japan in which people felt insecure about their future but also felt freer than they did when, in the Showa era, moving around to seek employment was equated with being unsuccessful in a single steady job, as well as with being "bad for the children." Needless to say, with the exception of the rich, people had many fewer possessions than they do now. You could pack a few suitcases and move house rather easily. Now you need a huge moving truck to take all the "stuff" you and your family "need." Japan in the Meiji era was a much less materialistic society than it became after the Second World War. People were satisfied with far fewer things. Of course, poor people like Takuboku (and unlike Kenji, whose family was one of the wealthiest in Iwate) could not afford to buy possessions. If you look at the houses in which people live in the films of Ozu Yasujiro up until the time in the early 1950s when he started making films about more well-to-do people, they are almost empty. (What is seen by many people as a kind of "Zen-like" atmosphere in Ozu's sets is really due to the sparseness of things in people's lives at the time. It's easy to be a minimalist when you are poor.)

Takuboku might have returned to his hometown had he lived longer. His reputation even when he was alive was formidable. It was bound to grow. He could have moved back to Iwate with his family, maybe even taken up a teaching position in Morioka. But his life was not long, and he was destined to suffer for being away.

"Thoughts of home well in my heart like a sickness." This is how he sees his nostalgia for his hometown. They assault him like a recurring infection. But it is more than a sickness for home. It is a sickness for the innocence that he once had, for the ability to laugh and cry without being judged, for the freedom to express what he felt without fear of being censured.

That is what "hometown" means to Takuboku. The freedom to be himself again, a freedom he, who spent so much of his short adult life on the road, sadly never recaptured.

EVERY SINGLE NIGHT

I curl myself up to the corner
Of crowded trains.
It's what I admire most about myself.

The word Takuboku uses for "curl myself up" is *chijikomaru*. This word contains the nuance of making yourself both smaller and rounder. The image is one of a fetal position, where you are too small for people to notice you.

LYING ON MY BACK IN THE GRASS

A bird poos on my forehead out of the blue
Then takes to the sky.
Nothing in mind ...

In Italy and the culture of some other countries it is considered good luck when a bird poos on you. Takuboku might agree. At any rate, he has nothing particular on his mind when this happens, just like the bird. Perhaps he envies the bird that can just fly away and not think about its actions.

FOR NO PARTICULAR REASON

All I did was wave my hat
At the top of the tall mountain
Before setting back down again.

I translate *naniganashi* here with "for no particular reason," because I believe that Takuboku himself doesn't know why he walked up and down the mountain simply to wave his hat. It's not important whether he was waving to someone or not. The gesture itself is everything for him. He doesn't seem perturbed that he can't explain his actions to himself.

IN SOME WAYS

Coming to the outskirts of the city
Is like visiting the grave
Of the first person you fell for.

I chose "the first person you fell for" as a translation of *hatsukoibito*, which is usually rendered with "first love." The reason I chose this is the association of the verb "fall" with death. Takuboku uses an ancient word for "grave," *okutsuki*, a word that is recorded in the eighth century, not that long after the Japanese adopted the Chinese writing system for their language. This is a comment as much about Japanese cities, naturally much smaller in his day than they are today, as it is about how he feels when he makes an excursion out of them.

AT THE STATION

I slip into the crowd
Just to hear the accent
Of my faraway hometown.

This is one of Takuboku's most famous tanka. It shows just how nostalgic he was for his hometown. It also comments on the many people from Iwate, a poor region of Japan at the time, who went to Hokkaido, a "new land" of opportunity, to seek work, as Takuboku did. The mimetic word "slip" suggests that he joins the crowd without trying to be conspicuous. In fact, I sometimes think of Takuboku as a kind of invisible man, present at a place and a time, which he describes with perfect clarity, and yet is himself unseen—the perfect existence for an artist: to see and not be seen.

IN THE RUINS OF KOZUKATA CASTLE

I dozed off in the weeds
As the sky seized
My fifteen-year-old heart.

Twice in 2014, the year in which I translated the bulk of these tanka—in April and again in October—I sat under the tree in Iwate Park where there is a stone monument of this tanka in the hand of Takuboku's close friend, Kindaichi Kyosuke (see page thirty-three). I closed my eyes and tried to imagine Takuboku, age fifteen, sitting right there. When he was in middle school, he suddenly left the classroom during class and went to that very spot in the park (which was then and still is today the site of the ruins of Kozukata Castle) and sat under the tree there. It was while I was on that very spot a hundred and thirteen years later that I felt the urge and the inspiration to translate his work. I use "weeds" for *kusa*, which also means "grass," because this often suggests a lawn to a Western reader. In any case, *kusa* can also mean "herbs" and "flowers." "Weeds" is definitely what was there then. While "sucked into the sky" would have been a more literal translation of the original *sora ni suwareshi*, I chose to make the sky the subject of an active verb. This lends a dynamic feeling to the poem. In addition, "my heart was sucked into the sky" just doesn't sound as poetic in English as it does in Japanese.

AUTUMN WIND

The millet leaves flutter
Rustling along the eaves of home
Taking me back.

Hatahata, a mimetic word, comes out in the translation with two mimetic English words, "flutter" and "rustling." "Leaves" and "eaves" reinforce this imagery. It has often been said that English lacks an equivalent of the Japanese *natsukashisa*. This is, needless to say, not true. There are a number of ways to render this word into English. Here I have chosen the phrase "taking me back" ... something that takes you back to a former time or place. The adjective *natsukashii* can also be translated with "fondly remembered" or "recalled with nostalgia" or "conjuring up sweet memories."

MY HEART

My heart, sick beast
Is soothed by news
Of my old hometown.

It is said in English that "music has charms to soothe a savage beast." This is actually a quotation from "The Mourning Bride," a play written in 1697 by the English playwright and poet William Congreve. With Takuboku it is news of his hometown that soothes the beast in him. The verb "to soothe" is a beautiful sounding one in English. The original has a lovely lyrical quality, with his heart (*kokoro*) being made silent and calm (*otonashi*) by what he hears of his old hometown.

ASAKUSA

Nothing isolates me more
Than slipping in and out of
Merry nighttime crowds.

Asakusa, with its theaters and craft works, was a much greater hub of entertainment and culture in Takuboku's time than it is now. Even Miyazawa Kenji, solitary goody-two-shoes that he was, used to love going there to see theater and, in his day, moving pictures ... and to buy racy woodblock prints. Again, Takuboku's sense of isolation in a crowd is evident in this tanka.

A HABIT

I casually and aimlessly leave home.
I casually and abruptly return.
And all my friend can do is laugh.

Hyozen-to appears twice in this tanka, emphasizing Takuboku's attitude. I wasn't sure how best to convey this adverb in English. It can be "abruptly" or "aimlessly," as well as "casually." Somehow no single one of these seemed to fit the mood and message of this tanka, so I chose to use all three. I don't think Takuboku himself knows why he has this habit.

THE TRAIN

I hear a distant whistle.
It lingers in the air before vanishing
Into woods.

Naganaga-to hibikasete ("to sound for a long time") is expressed by the whistle that lingers. The origin of the word "linger" is the same as that of the words "long" and "lengthen," which is the root of the Japanese word as well. The movement of the train itself can be visualized in this metaphor of sound.

SEEING OFF AT THE TRAIN STATION

My wife came with our daughter on her back.
I caught sight of her eyebrows
Through a blanket of snow.

Even though it is snowing heavily, Setsuko still comes to the station with their daughter on her back to see him off. I chose the metaphor of a blanket of snow, which is not literally in the original, because a blanket is something which covers people who love each other. The visual power of Takuboku's tanka comes out here, with only a mere glimpse of her eyebrows remaining for him.

MOVING HOUSE

Her photographs, photographs I'd forgotten
Lay at my feet
On the morning of leaving.

Takuboku uses the word *shashin* (photograph) twice. That's how important these photographs are—or were—to him. But will he bother to pick up them up before he moves to a new home?

IN MY MIND'S EYE

I weep for the willows
With their tender young leaves
On the banks of my river at home.

This famous tanka speaks of Takuboku's nostalgia for the landscape in Shibutami. There is a tall stone monument in Shibutami with this tanka carved into it. I chose "weep" instead of "cry" because English (and some other European languages) has the term "weeping willow." I left out the name of the river, the Kitakami, which appears in the original, because it simply didn't fit into the flow of the poem in English; and used "my river at home" instead. He is weeping for his lost childhood as much as for the trees on the bank.

IN MY GARDEN

Smashing my watch on a boulder
Brought back all the sweetness
Of long-lost anger.

Takuboku's personality was volatile, and that volatility is illustrated in this tanka. Sometimes Takuboku's volatility is paradoxical, giving rise to strong mixed feelings. I very rarely lose my temper, but once, in a fit of anger, I did and smashed a watch on the floor. I don't look back at it as *itoshii* (fondly), however, as Takuboku does here. Incidentally, Takuboku apparently never smashed his watch. He probably only wanted to. The mimetic sense of *hatato* ("suddenly" or "completely") in the original is expressed in the first word of the translation, "smashing." *Hatato* usually acts as an emphasizer of a verb, such as in "hitting on" an idea or "stopping short" of doing something, instead of just "getting" an idea or "ceasing" to do something. Takuboku is evidently savoring memories of youthful anger and, perhaps, regretting his inability to conjure it up as an adult.

AS IF ILL

Smoke drifting across a blue sky
Transports me back home.
And I suffer for it.

The translation has Takuboku being "transported back home" (another way of rendering *natsukashisa*) on drifting smoke. Almost anything he catches sight of can remind him instantly of the heartache of being a drifter himself.

AN AVENUE OF TREES

My diary will tell how I was drawn
To the black locusts and poplars
As they swayed sadly in the autumn wind.

When he says that he has left something in his diary, he means it not only as a record of how he felt on that day but as one meant for us to read for many years in the future. This was definitely in Takuboku's mind. The black locust tree is also called a yellow or false acacia. It was introduced to Japan in the early Meiji era and has spread throughout the entire country, from Hokkaido in the north to the islands of Okinawa in the south.

JAPANESE ROSE

Will you flower again this year, Japanese rose
In the sand dunes of the northern beach
Fragrant with the tide?

Hamanasu (or *hamanashi*) is a Japanese flower of the rose family with red petals (or, more rarely, white) and a strong fragrance. The fragrance of tide and rose merge beautifully in this tanka. You can almost smell them together as you think of Takuboku's loneliness on his northern beach.

THREE-STORY BUILDING

A spring snow
Is falling gently against bricks
On a Ginza backstreet.

Some of Takuboku's tanka paint a realistic portrait of Japan in the last years of the Meiji era, which corresponded with the last years of his life. This portrait of what was then a tall building on a Ginza backstreet is very evocative of the era; and the contrast of the soft snow against the hard brick is stark and illustrative of that concreteness of image that I mentioned in the Preface. Bricks were often used in construction up to the time of the Great Kanto Earthquake of 1923, when many brick buildings fell down. This tanka, of course, was written years before the earthquake. But even in Takuboku's time the Ginza was Tokyo's premier district of fashion and modernity.

ON A TRAIN

I glanced out the window on a rainy night
To catch the clock at a station
Stopped in the woods.

Kenji no doubt knew this tanka, which seems almost like a little scene out of *Night on the Milky Way Train*. The image of the clock stopped as the train seems to continue going past this station in the woods strikes me as one that would have inspired Kenji. The rich suggestiveness of Takuboku's tanka is evident here: Is it the train or the clock that has stopped? Poetic words in haiku and tanka are said to possess *fukurami* (literally, "swelling"). This means that the image continues to grow, with a life of its own, outside the bounds of the word or words that create it. Takuboku is a master at generating this "swelling" in the spare thirty-one syllables of a tanka.

ARRIVING LATE AT NIGHT AT THE STATION

The man couldn't keep still.
So before long he simply walked out
Without his hat on.

It was unusual in that era to go out without a hat on, in the West as well as in Westernizing Japan. It is unclear if this man is Takuboku or someone he observed. Either way, he identifies with the sense of being "directionless" in an era of social unrest. The mundane quality of this tanka is typical of many poems in this genre. They are about the little dramas of every day.

FROM THE SECOND STORY

A child is observing comings and goings
Forgetting all about the sweets
Coming to her.

This is a portrait of Takuboku's daughter, who is more fascinated by the people she observes than by the candy she might be receiving. Takuboku is describing the procession of humanity before a fascinated observer. Could it be that he is hoping that his daughter will share his observational powers someday? "Coming to her," of course, has the double meaning of sweets that she will receive and those she has a right to receive.

FOR THE FIRST TIME IN A LONG TIME

My pillow was carried to the edge of the verandah
So that the stars
Would get to me.

Shitashimeru is a difficult word to translate, with its denotation of "being able to become close to or intimate with." I have chosen "get to me" because of its two meanings: "to move me" and "to reach me."

MY HOMETOWN

I face the mountains
speechless.
I owe those mountains everything.

Another of Takuboku's most well-read and quoted tanka. He says about his feelings: *iukotonashi*, which literally means "having nothing to say." Despite the fact that he says a lot of things about the mountains of home, this is, however paradoxical, very indicative of his feelings about them. There is no way to express the depth of his emotion except to say that there is no way. Much later, iconoclastic author Sakaguchi Ango, who was from Niigata on the Sea of Japan coast, said something similar: *Furusato wa/Kataru koto nashi.* Literally this means: "There is nothing I can say about my hometown." Ango's saying, however, has a much more ironical slant to it. Unlike Takuboku, he hated the place he came from. As for *arigataki* in this tanka, "grateful" or "thankful" would be acceptable translations. But not here. Takuboku's response to his hometown is more absolute. Without them he would not be the creative person he is … or at least he implicitly believed that.

CITY STREETS

I am suddenly struck by an urge
The urge to walk along every street
Through the dead of night.

I have translated *omoi wakikinu* (literally, "the notion welling up, gushing up in me") with "struck by an urge." I feel that "urge" is an appropriate word to describe something in Takuboku's psyche. He is often impulsive; and this impulsive quality strikes him at all hours of the day and night. Of course, acting on this urge is a different matter. More often than not, he is content to describe it and leave it at that.

THE TRIP

And so another year has passed
Picturing myself in a new suit
Going far away.

The key visual image here is that of the new suit, as if a new suit of clothes might help a man start a new life or have new adventures somewhere away from home. Again, words and images; no action. He at least knows this well about himself.

WITHOUT A THOUGHT

I hopped onto a train
But jumped off at a station
Unable to move backward or forward.

The words "hopped onto" and "jumped off" emphasize the impulsiveness of the actions that were taken "for some reason or other" (*nantonaku*).

SICK DREAMS

Five years have gone by
Since I left my old hometown
And yet the cuckoo still cries in my dreams.

The cuckoo comes back to haunt him, reminding him of the passage of time and the shortness of life. The cry of this bird, the *kankodori* or *kakko*, whose name is mimetic in Japanese as it is in English, has commonly appeared in haiku and tanka for centuries as a symbol of longing, of missing a place, or of emptiness.

NEVER FAR

I miss the mountains of Shibutami.
I miss the rivers of Shibutami.
They are never far from my mind.

This is another one of Takuboku's popular tanka about Shibutami. "Never far" implies that in his mind and heart he has never really left Shibutami.

LEAVING MY OLD HOMETOWN

I am grief stricken forever
As if pursued by men
With stones in their hands.

There is something biblical about the imagery in this tanka, as when someone is about to be stoned to death. That's why I chose the word "stricken," which comes from "strike." Takuboku's leaving home bordered on the traumatic for him. The pathos is in the word "forever," that this feeling will be with him until the day he dies.

MY YOUTH

The spirit of my youth
Has taken flight unfettered
Like a kite whose string has been cut away.

This tanka expresses a lovely metaphor, indicating both the delight and the fear of
freedom of the young person leaving home, of not being "tied down."

BALL

Ages ago I threw a ball
Up to the elementary school shingled roof.
I wonder where it is now.

The old school still stands in Shibutami just beside his memorial museum. When I
first went there, the first thing I did was stand on tiptoes to look on top of the sloping
roof to see if I could see a ball there.

WHISTLING

I don't whistle anymore
Even in my dreams.
Whistling was my poetry when I was fifteen.

Whistling is a symbol of personal freedom and being carefree. Takuboku can't even dream of himself doing that anymore.

RECOMMENDATION

A friend recommended Tokutomi's histories to me.
But he was too poor
To continue his studies.

In Takuboku's day, as in ours, some people are unable to move to a higher level of education due to financial difficulties. Takuboku reminds us of this reality for many people in this tanka with its keen social message. Tokutomi Soho was a famous scholar and politician who was born twenty-three years before Takuboku. He long outlived Takuboku, dying at the age of ninety-four.

CARES

It happened one day.
I changed the paper on the sliding doors.
My cares flew away that day.

The word "cares" naturally refers both to worries and, by nuance, things to care about. Takuboku was a man with both lots of cares and lots of things to care about. Perhaps on this one day, all cares flew out the window when he was changing its paper, and he felt like he might be able to start things all over again.

MEMORIES

There are also memories
That give you a weird feeling
The feeling you get when putting on dirty socks.

A witty comparison tied to everyday life. Takuboku finds much poetry in the mundane and the banal. This, of course, is a traditional poetic outlook that goes back centuries in Japan.

RAIN

The rain in the capital conjures
The rain that falls equally
On the pale purple potato flowers of home.

The rain is something that brings together the place he is physically in, Tokyo, and the place his heart resides in, Shibutami. The contrast between the big city and the countryside is stark. It exists within him all the time and is the cause of his heartache and the source of his inspiration.

PART THREE

Society Politics Work

The Meiji era has often been misunderstood in Japan. There is a reason for this: The imperialism and emperor worship established as national policy in that era morphed into a brutal and racist militarism. This threw opinions about that era in and outside Japan into a very dim and horrific light.

On a trip to London in April 2014 to deliver a speech about the possible future place of Japan in the world, I visited the old bookshops at Leicester Square, as I always do when I am in that city. The first thing I do is ask the people in the shops if they have anything relating to Japan. They sometimes produce lithographs or etchings from the Meiji era.

On this particular trip, the owner of a little pop-up stall, the kind you see at book fairs in Japan, showed me a color lithograph in excellent condition. It depicted a man on horseback in military uniform wearing a hat with a tall white plume. Both the man and the horse are staring straight out at the person holding the picture. Below the man and horse is a map of East Asia. The horse stands in a rearing pose. Its right back hoof is firmly planted in northern China; the left back hoof stands on top of Formosa, the name at the time for Taiwan.

Its front legs are about to come down on other parts of Asia.

I recognized the man on the horse before reading the caption below the picture. It is Emperor Meiji, known in the West by his name, Mutsuhito. And sure enough, the caption reads: "The Mikado, Mutsu Hito, Emperor of Japan (b. 1852)." The rest of the longish caption goes on to state, in part …

> *The Mikado is represented in the dress of Commander-in-Chief of the Japanese Army, and is seated upon a charger which supports itself partly upon Manchuria, Mongolia, and Formosa. One leg rests firmly upon Formosa, gained by the Japanese after the war of 1895, and much improved by them. … The energy displayed by Japan during the present conflict indicates that she intends to neglect no chance of strengthening her foothold on the continent.*

The "present conflict" is the Russo-Japanese War, and I would date this lithograph to sometime in mid-1904.

But the most telling statement in the picture is the title in bold capital letters at the top …

ENGLAND'S FRIEND IN THE FAR EAST

It has been forgotten by many people that the Western powers applauded Japanese moves into China and Korea. As far as the British were concerned, this would weaken Russian power and allow them to strengthen and expand their domain in Central Asia and regions around the Black Sea.

Well, what, you may ask, does all this have to do with a collection of tanka by Ishikawa Takuboku? The answer is that it is crucial. The society that Takuboku was a part of and took an active interest in was in high political flux. It was an era of high polemics. Intellectuals and socially conscious people were actively involved in a nationwide discussion, played out in all aspects of the culture—literature, theater, graphic arts, journalism—as to what the nature of future Japanese society should be. Basically, it is the same discussion that continues to go on today not only in Japan but in many countries around the world: Should society be open to ideas on the basis of their true merit, creating a fluid situation that leads to the betterment of all classes? Or should the body polity be unified in thought and action behind one ethnic (or religious) idea, an idea that presumably makes the nation "stronger" and more successful at engaging in conflicts with other countries?

As we all know, Japan chose the latter scenario—with both "pure" Japanese ethnicity and the native Shinto religion to "legitimize" it—and the brilliant and multi-faceted culture of the late Meiji era (Takuboku's times) and the Taisho era was flung into the gutter and stamped on with thick-soled mud and blood-smeared boots. If Japanese people had chosen to follow the former path of open-ended development and freedom of expression, Japan, I believe, would have produced a culture that would have dazzled the world in all forms of cultural, social and political expression.

Of course, it was not only Japan that abandoned freedom for the alleged glories of unity. Germany and Russia (then the Soviet Union) did the same. Germany lost many thousands of creative liberal people who chose expatriation. They also lost almost all of their most talented scientists, some of whom went to the United States and worked on the development of the atomic bomb. Russia lost, primarily by murdering them, some of the greatest writers and other intellectuals that the modern world had known. And Stalin eliminated some of his best generals not long before he would need them to do battle with Germany.

It is clear that Takuboku identified in his writing with those people who wanted fervently to reform Japanese society. In fact, he identified so much so that he himself wished to be a part of the movement. Sadly, in his own eyes, he lacked the resolve to commit himself. Perhaps "resolve" is not the right word. Perhaps he was simply like most people in any country. They sympathize with the reformers but are too bogged down in the troubles of their own everyday life to be able to extricate themselves from them. Takuboku was like a man caught in quicksand, not sinking further down but yet unable to get out. He pulls his own hair up, hoping that this will somehow extricate him. But it just causes further pain and anguish, with the result that he remains where he is, struggling just to keep his arms and feet moving, to "keep afloat."

In his life Takuboku identified with the downtrodden because he saw himself as one of them. In his *Diary in Roman Letters* he writes about how desperately he is in need of money. Life for him, with a wife, daughter and mother to support, was a constant struggle for survival. He could look back, however, to a much more comfortable childhood, with his father being chief priest at a temple. Perhaps his desperation at being poor was exacerbated by memories of such a childhood.

In the Heisei era that ended in 2019 and now is the Reiwa era, with the ever-widening gap between the haves and the have-nots, this struggle for survival has become a reality for more and more Japanese people. The lack of job security that plagued Takuboku's life, the necessity to move from place to place wherever there was a job to be had, the anxiety caused by the fact that a person could be fired at the drop of a hat for "not fitting in" or for arguing against injustice, the introduction of restrictions on freedom, the oppression of people seen by the government as "radical" … these aspects of Takuboku's times have become all too familiar in today's Japan.

This is what makes Takuboku our contemporary. And though he may have found himself unable to act, he participated in the polemics through his writing, demonstrating to us the importance of free expression, of dialogue and argument, of commitment in the public arena to asserting the rights of all people.

There are two crucial historical events occurring in Takuboku's lifetime that affected him deeply. The first is the attempt on the part of Tanaka Shozo to hand a petition to Emperor Meiji to do something about the toxic waste produced by the Ashio Copper Mine that was polluting the waters at farms downstream in Tochigi Prefecture. Though Takuboku was only fifteen at the time of this incident (December 1901), it impacted his consciousness sufficiently for him to write a tanka about it.

Tanaka Shozo was one of the world's first ecological pioneers. Not only an amazing social thinker who formulated his own principles of *nagare* (flow) and *doku* (poison) to highlight the vital importance of protecting nature from manmade pollution, but also a progressive intellectual and agitator who, as editor of the daily Ibaraki Shimbun (today's Shimono Shimbun) propagated the works of John Stuart Mill and Jeremy Bentham. He was elected to the Diet in 1890, which itself shows that Japanese democracy was sufficiently developed to accommodate such a visionary in the "establishment."

I was reminded of the 1901 petition to the emperor event when Diet member Yamamoto Taro handed an anti-nuclear letter to the emperor in 2013, exactly a century after the death of Tanaka Shozo; and I was dismayed at the vilification poured on Yamamoto by the media for his breaking of protocol. Not much has changed in a century. Perhaps in some ways Meiji Japan was more tolerant of dissent than today's Japan.

Just one more note on Tanaka Shozo, a quotation of something he said that rings true today ...

A true civilization does not destroy mountains, does not destroy rivers, does not tear apart villages, does not murder people.

If any quotation from the Meiji era proves that the issues in which Takuboku and his contemporaries were deeply and personally involved are no different from those that affect us today, this one does. A society without vigorous evidence-based polemics that reach the public through various forms of media is a society destined to stagnate.

The second incident affecting Takuboku, to an even greater degree, was that concerning the socialist author, translator and journalist Kotoku Shusui, who was arrested for treason on trumped-up charges in what became known as "the Daigyaku Jiken," or "High Treason Incident," and executed together with others on 24 January 1911. This date has to be seen as marking the beginning of the decline of Japanese democracy, a decline that took Japan down the dark spiral staircase to hell, ending in the defeat in war on 15 August 1945.

The cause and fate of Shusui had a huge impact on Takuboku. For one thing, he was much older than he had been when encountering the cause of Tanaka Shozo back in 1901. For another, Tanaka was certainly not executed, and was allowed to continue writing.

Both Shusui and Takuboku were passionate followers of the writings of the Russian scientist, philosopher and anarchist Pyotr Kropotkin. Like Shusui, Takuboku had read Kropotkin's work in English. On 15 June 1911, less than half a year after Shusui's execution, he wrote the long poem titled "After Endless Argument" in which he bemoaned the lack of activism in Japan. In it he quotes the Russian exhortation, *V narod!*

V narod! is a call to action that has its roots in the middle of the nineteenth century, primarily as a feature of the anti-feudal philosophy of the Russian socialist Aleksandr Herzen. The principle was *narodnichestvo*, which means "unity with the people." The activists and progressives who held this belief were called Narodniki, and they advocated that activists of all sorts should "V narod!" ie, "Go to the people!" This, in a nutshell, is the philosophical, if vague, basis of Takuboku's ideal of activism.

Yet despite his belief, he found himself unable to become an active protester, and he had pangs of conscience over this personal shortcoming. Even so, his honesty shines through. He admits his shortcomings and continues to support progressive people through his writing. In this sense, he *is* an activist by way of his self-searching introspection, which has the ring of truth to us today.

As far as employment was concerned, Takuboku traveled from Iwate to Tokyo, Otaru and Hakodate, and to Sapporo and Kushiro, but was not able to secure long-term work on what might be called a decent salary today. Takuboku and his family lived, of necessity, a very frugal life. Sometimes, when he did receive a lump sum from a publisher, it didn't last long. His son was born in October 1910. On the day of the birth, he was paid twenty yen (about a month's wage) by the publisher of his tanka collection, *A Handful of Sand*. But the boy died on the twenty-seventh of that month, and the royalty went to pay for the funeral.

In his work, Takuboku was not often able to pursue his ideas and get them into the public eye in the form of journalism. For a time he was relegated to the job of proofreader, which left him feeling frustrated and unfulfilled.

The great lesson that we learn from the life and writing of Takuboku is this: A society either creates a place for its creative people to be freely active in the way they see fit, or that society will go into decline and cease to prosper.

In the decades following the death of Takuboku, the country closed its doors to free expression, persecuting, tormenting, torturing and, in some cases, murdering its free thinkers. This was bound to bring Japan to the brink of self-inflicted disaster.

HUNGER

Do not despise the beggar
For his baseness, my friend.
I too once sunk as low.

Takuboku is never above self-criticism. He identified with the disadvantaged and downtrodden in society. There is no doubt in my mind that, had he lived into the 1930s and early 1940s, he would have been considered a dangerous element by the government. His popularity would not have protected him.

THE NASTY CARPENTER'S SON

It's saddening. Among many
The young man went to war
To come back dead.

Opinion is divided as to whether it is the carpenter or his son who is nasty. The English phrase "nasty carpenter's son" leaves the question just as open as does *ijiwaru no daiku no ko* in Japanese. *Ikite kaerazu* would normally be translated with "not return alive," but I find this kind of literal translation unsatisfactory; so I chose "to come back dead." It also carries the possible nuance that the boy actually may have gone to war in order to come back dead, that is, to be a dead hero.

ASSASSINATION

I wish someone would shoot me like they shot Ito
And let me die
A death like his.

The reference here is to Ito Hirobumi, four-time prime minister of Japan and resident-general of Korea. He was shot and killed in October 1909 by An Jung-geun, who is considered a national hero in Korea.

BELIEF

I believe in the new age.
My belief and my word
Are one ... yet.

The key word is *shinzu*, "to believe." He believes that he is a man who tells the truth, but self-doubt lurks within his belief. Again, Takuboku displays a modern psychological sensibility, like a character in the fiction of Franz Kafka.

FROM THE SIDELINES

Everybody is proceeding in one direction
Save for a single mind
That solely watches.

Takuboku wants to join the crowd, especially if it is marching toward a progressive future. But his role, it seems, turns out to be that of the passive observer who perpetually sits on the sidelines and comments on the action.

LABOR

However long I work
Life remains a trial.
I just stare into my palms.

This is another well-known tanka that Japanese study in school. It is one of Takuboku's iconic statements about the life of a working person. Life is, to him, a trial, and I chose this English word carefully, rather than just say that life is not easy, which is close to the original Japanese. It is a trial in which you are asked, "What will you do about it?" Takuboku's answer here seems to be just to contemplate his situation by staring into his hands. He wants to do more but, by temperament, he finds it a trial to do so. He is also identifying here with the working class, whose hands are worn and rough from toil.

REGIMENT OFF TO WAR

I stand on the sidelines to see them go
Grieving
For their collectedness.

Takuboku lived through both the Sino-Japanese War (1894-95) and the Russo-Japanese War (1904-05), conflicts that defined the new role of Japan, for better and for worse, in Asia. At the time, however, it was almost universally thought of as for the better, not only in Japan but in Europe and America as well. The Western powers fully supported Japan's new role in Asia. But in this tanka, Takuboku is somewhat circumspect, and he is grieving (he uses a form of the word that appears so often in his writing, *kanashii*). The word "collectedness" here expresses what he is sad about: that the departing soldiers are all together in a group; and that they are composed and calm ... even though many may not come back.

SHORT SHRIFT

Hey, they wrote up my poems
In this old newspaper
But commended them in only a few short lines.

Takuboku was very ambitious. He believed in his talent; and that is a good thing. I like the use of *oya* (hey) here. It sounds a bit ironical, or perhaps more accurately, sarcastic. There is another irony here too. After all, Takuboku's poems are only a few lines long. Why should people praise them in more lines than their length?

PATHETIC

What a pathetic morning spent picking misprints
Off the pages of the hometown newspaper
Spread before me!

Takuboku spent many a tedious day proofing newspaper articles. Here it's his hometown paper that he's reading. I've translated the form of *kanashii* that he uses here with "pathetic," because obviously he is feeling not only sad but sorry for himself.

FIRST THING IN THE MORNING

An article about a homeless old man
Moved me to tears
Not long after I opened my eyes.

Takuboku, being a newspaperman and a Meiji intellectual, is wedded to reading the paper in the morning, just like people today turn on their smart phones the minute they wake up to find out what "the news" is. Here, he senses, he could almost be reading an article about himself in the future.

A FIND

I slipped my hand into a sand dune.
As I dug in, my fingers touched
A pistol crusted in rust.

He is putting an image in the reader's mind here that begs the question (to the reader and to himself): What will be the next move?

BARE FACE

I break out in a cold sweat
Over how often I lied.
How I lied with a bare face.

I translated *heiki nite yoku uso o iiki* (to unashamedly tell lies) by modifying the lies with "bare face." This, after all, is where the sweat makes his shame—or fear—evident.

INDELIBLE INK

I hear the autumn wind blowing
As I blacken in
A map of Korea.

Another tanka that gives an impression of his era, when Japan was colonizing Korea and painting its colonies red on the map. Takuboku's attitude toward this colonization is clear here. (The tanka on page seventy-five also contains a reference to Korea, because Ito Hirobumi was assassinated by a Korean nationalist.)

THE NEW YEAR

Will this year be like all others
With my mind conjuring only things
That the world will not accept?

Takuboku realized, as did Kenji, that he was out of step with his era. Had he lived longer, into the Showa era, he might have found himself even more at odds with Japanese society, as it turned triumphant imperialism into a militaristic nightmare. These things that "the world will not accept" may very well be aspects of the personal, things that have to do with his desires.

FUMES

It gives me no joy to turn my gaze
To my garden turning green
While my eyes sting from the fumes of fresh ink.

I have chosen to translate the form of the word *kanashii* with "it gives me no joy" rather than the more usual "it makes me sad." Sometimes the best translation is a grammatical negation: turning the positive into a negative coupled with a word of the opposite meaning; or into a positive, if the phrase in the original is in the negative. I did the latter when I translated Kenji's most famous poem, "Ame ni mo Makezu" (literally, "not giving in to the rain") with "strong in the rain." I didn't use smell or odor for *nioi* because in English an odor itself cannot sting the eyes. It has to be the fumes of the odor. In addition, the alliterative "fumes of fresh ink" has a beautiful sound in English. This is an intriguing tanka. Takuboku is obviously eager to write with his fresh ink. Should he be looking at the blank paper or his blooming garden?

ON MY WAY TO WORK

A sudden change of heart takes me
To the river bank
Where I spend another aimless day.

Once again we see the volatility of his whims. This whim takes him to the bank of a river. He wanders up and down it (using the word "roam, wander," *samayoeri*), which I have rendered with "aimless." Is it any wonder that some of his colleagues and bosses fell out with him?

PRISONERS

Every individual is a prisoner
Of the self. The heart cries out
Forlorn.

To be "forlorn" is another highly suggestive English way of translation *kanashisa*, the noun that means "sadness." The kanji for person or individual, *hito*, appears four times in this tanka. This repetition emphasizes Takuboku's message that all of us are ruled by our subconscious self. Takuboku here anticipates one aspect of twentieth-century psychology, according to which people can be seen as being their own worst enemy.

SOMEWHERE OR OTHER

There's a horde of people drawing lots.
It's my lot
To be drawn to them.

I've chosen to create a play on words with the two meanings of "lot." This is in the spirit of the original, in which there is also a play on words in the use of the verb "to draw." There is a feeling in this tanka that the events of one's life and fate are as capricious as a lottery.

REVOLUTION

Nothing seems to disconcert my wife and friends
More than my going on about revolution
Even when struck down by illness.

Takuboku has the ability to see himself through the eyes of others. This is a rare ability in a human being and one we should admire in him. He became increasingly radicalized in the last years and, had he lived to see it, no doubt would have welcomed the Russian revolution, even though he expressed strong anti-Russian sentiments during the Russo-Japanese War.

THE TERRORIST

I had thought it remote from me
But now see how close it can feel …
The sad mind of the terrorist.

The contrast that sets the tone of this tanka is the words "remote" and "close." The mind of the terrorist is a thing that Takuboku understood because he knew that he shared some of the terrorists' values. The meaning of the word "terrorist" was somewhat different to what it is today. In Takuboku's day, terrorists directed their violence against a person or persons they considered cruel enemies. By and large, they didn't deal in indiscriminate violence.

JUST ONCE

I wonder what it would feel like
To do just one wicked thing
And act as if you hadn't done it.

In this and the two succeeding tanka, Takuboku speaks of himself as a man of inaction with regret. In this one, he even has a vision of himself as an active terrorist.

DYNAMOS

The loud roar of the dynamos pleases me.
If only I could sound off
Like that.

Here Takuboku regrets that his "voice" in society is too quiet. The working image here is of industrialization. The years of his life correspond with a spectacular reinvention of Japan into a modern industrialized state.

SMOKE

I never tire of following smoke
As it twirls up
Vanishing like a dragon into an empty sky.

In this one he speaks of the fact that he spends so much time observing. Again, factory smoke, a symbol of the new Japan.

ALL THE THINGS

Had I only been the editor
Of the paper ... all the things
I once thought I could do!

Takuboku was once an editor, when he worked for a short time at the Kushiro Shimbun in Hokkaido. But in Tokyo at the Asahi, the major daily, he was, alas, just a proofreader.

PART FOUR

Illness Death

Perhaps the most difficult thing for us to understand about life a century and longer ago is the people's attitude toward illness and death. People generally had many children, because it was assumed that they would lose some of them before they reached adulthood. And many highly contagious diseases, such as tuberculosis, polio and influenza affected people of all nations and social classes.

My mother, born in the year that Takuboku died, 1912, was one of four children in a very wealthy household. She and her siblings were taken around in a chauffeur-driven car, and they had a live-in governess. But the youngest sibling, my uncle Joe, caught polio as a child and walked with a limp throughout his life. He was lucky to survive. My mother's elder sister, my aunt Helen, contracted pneumonia and died, age twenty-nine, in November 1937. As I was born in 1944, I know her only through a few photographs.

My father, born in New York City in 1903, was seventeen years younger than Takuboku and only seven years younger than Kenji. He told me how he used to watch the vegetable peddler take an apple from his cart and spit on it to polish it up before selling it. It had been known since the end of the nineteenth century that spitting spread tubercular germs, but this practice in public continued to be common in the U.S. until well after the middle of the twentieth century. When I first arrived in Japan in 1967, I often saw men spit in the street and even in train stations. This is one sure way to increase the infection rate of any number of illnesses.

The list of famous writers who died from tuberculosis is long, including Balzac, Camus, Thoreau, Chekhov, Kafka, D.H. Lawrence and George Orwell, to name a few. In Japan, the three great poets spanning the Meiji and Taisho eras—Shiki, Takuboku and Kenji—all died of it. It was the AIDS of its day.

And so, people in Takuboku's time were much more fatalistic about illness and death than we are today. We now tend to believe that grave illness is avoidable, and that death can be "cheated" or at least kept at bay for as long as possible. And we often blame others when they fall seriously ill: "It's their own fault for overeating or smoking or not exercising...." In Takuboku's day few people would have entertained such notions. If you fell ill, it couldn't be helped. If you died a premature death, it was, to many, "God's will."

Drugs and medical practices often did more harm to patients than good. Takuboku took a drug called Pyramidon for his tuberculosis. This was a kind of anti-inflammatory drug that, needless to say, did not cure the disease. In fact, its side effects on the immune system could be serious; and in 1936 it was officially designated as a poison in Britain.

While it is not possible to make a certain diagnosis of Takuboku's mental state, I do believe that he suffered from a form of depression. He definitely was enervated by insomnia and what Winston Churchill, another person with depression, called, in a metaphorical reference to his disease, "the black dog." (Actually, while this metaphor is often credited to Churchill, it was used much earlier, in the eighteenth century, by Samuel Johnson, who equally suffered from depression.)

Takuboku was also one who feigned illness, as if this would give grounding to his intense feelings of self-pity. As if this weren't enough of an excuse to stay away from work, he inflicted self-harm on himself by cutting his chest with a razor, but thankfully was stopped by his friend Kindaichi Kyosuke from doing himself serious harm. Kindaichi, ever the compassionate companion, pawned his overcoat and took the sulking Takuboku out for a tempura dinner accompanied by a lot of alcohol.

During his long stays in the hospital, Takuboku's world simply shrank. He could no longer roam city streets at night or feel the wind against his face. Being indoors for long periods, his world became limited by the confines of his room, the "long corridor" he writes about, and the glimpses of the outside that he gets from a window. Visits to the hospital by members of his family are special but awkward, as they can be in such circumstances. After all, Setsuko too had tuberculosis; and she was forced to carry on with her household duties even when debilitated and unable to breathe properly.

Takuboku, from time to time, exhibits what is called in modern psychiatry a "death wish." This is a desire to die that is expressed often, particularly in olden times, in romantic or heroic imagery. Many people saw a young death as somehow "beautiful." Why not, for after all there were many of them. You may as well idealize young death if you are going to witness it everywhere you look. Children who died were called "little angels."

Takuboku idealizes the death of people he sees as political martyrs. If only he himself could die such a death instead of just wasting away! But if we look behind this, more deeply into his psyche, we see that there are serious signs of the kind of depression that triggers a death wish, particularly withdrawal from human contact and self-reproach.

Isn't this precisely what we see in the Japan a century after Takuboku, people who shy away from human contact, withdraw into themselves and tend to blame themselves, often erupting in sudden anger? Takuboku expressed these feelings with intense honesty earlier than any other poet in Japan.

Other modern Japanese writers have exhibited a death wish, a wish that, unlike Takuboku, they carried out, all famous authors: Akutagawa Ryunosuke and Arishima Takeo; Dazai Osamu, Mishima Yukio and Kawabata Yasunari. But these death wishes differ in the methods the writers chose to take their lives. They all experienced a profound despair, either over their personal condition or the state of society as they saw it (the latter is particularly strong in Mishima's case). But none of these writers analyzed their condition or state of mind with the forthright candor that we see in the writing of Takuboku.

Takuboku is a model to us not only for this candor but also for his insight into his own psyche and his willingness to share it with us. There is nothing cunning or calculating about him; and if such a tendency does show up, he is the first to recognize it and shine a bright light on it.

He does have his dark moments. But it is the light piercing the darkness, not the absolute darkness, that reaches us today.

THE SHOT

That gunshot from the depths of the woods ...
Oh no, someone's killed himself.
From the sound it could be me.

Takuboku wrote this tanka in April 1909, when he was living in the Hongo district of Tokyo not far from an arsenal. Perhaps it was sounds coming from there that elicited these dark associations in his mind.

BY ALL RIGHTS

I smash one bowl whenever I am angry.
By all rights I should die
When I reach nine hundred and ninety-nine.

There is a distinct tone of absurdity here, and absurdity is often an element in Takuboku's tanka. Within this somewhat droll message, there is much self-knowledge concerning his temper and temperament.

MEDICINE

If only there were a medicine, light green
That made a man who drank it
Transparent, like water.

Takuboku wrote many tanka about illness. He spent much time in the company of doctors and nurses, all of whom were helpless in the face of his disease.

TOOTHACHE

I held my aching tooth in place
As I watched the sun rise blood red
Dripping through the winter mist.

Takuboku likens something happening inside his body to a phenomenon outside it, that is, in nature. I have chosen to translate *akaaka*, the repetition, for emphasis, of the character for "red" with "blood red," because it is blood, metaphorically, that is "dripping" through the mist, as blood drips out of gums in the mouth when a tooth is about to fall out. The last line of the tanka has a lyrical lilt to it in the original Japanese.

WORTH

"Worth dying for?"
"Worth living for?"
Not worth asking.

There is a lot of repetition in this tanka, and this makes its message come out strongly. It is Takuboku's way of interpreting young Hamlet's famous six words of monologue, "to be or not to be." In this tanka Takuboku takes this line from Shakespeare one step further. Is he an existentialist long before existentialism was formulated in the West?

AT A LOSS

I could not find the words
To reply to the doctor's
"Intent on dying, are you?"

Takuboku is describing his own feelings of despair through the comment of another person, in this case a doctor. The colloquial quality of the doctor's question in the original makes it seem very real. Takuboku uses a lot of traditional poetic turns of phrase in his tanka. But this question is posed in Japanese speech that is used exactly the same as today.

THE PATIENT

One push of the door, a single step
And the corridor seems to stretch
As far as the eye can see.

Anyone who has been in hospital with a serious illness will share Takuboku's sentiments and know how helpless one feels. Distances are defined on the basis of your physical state.

THE PATIENT

I called out to him but he didn't answer.
When I took a good look
The patient in the next bed was weeping.

This tanka and the succeeding three emphasize how important the experience in hospital was for Takuboku. When you are convalescing, you often lose your sense of the passage of time; you hear something and don't know what it signifies, such as a sound coming from the next bed. Here Takuboku shows much compassion for a fellow patient; someone like a nurse touches you and you are extremely sensitive to each touch and its "meaning"; and even seeing a policeman out the window is an event. These tanka are just as fresh today as they were more than a century ago.

IN THE HOSPITAL

Oh the joy of leaning out the window
And for the first time in ages
Catching sight of a policeman!

LATE AT NIGHT IN THE HOSPITAL

There's a commotion in one of the rooms.
Has someone died?
I hold my breath.

MY PULSE

The nurse's fingers on my pulse
Feel warm some days
And some days, cold and stiff.

SECRET WISH

If my illness got worse
The nurses would spend the night
Looking after me.

Meiji society was ruled by formalized social conventions, and it was not often that young men and women could meet and spend time together as they do now. It is known that quite a few Japanese people used to marry their cousins, as people do in many traditional societies, where encounters with strangers of the opposite sex are not very common. One of the times that young men and young women could meet and get to know each other was at weddings and funerals. It's not surprising that people married within extended families. It is also not surprising that Takuboku liked to be with his nurses. Even Miyazawa Kenji, whose works, unlike those of Takuboku, are almost entirely devoid of references to romantic love, fell in love with one of his nurses when, as a teenager, he was in a Morioka hospital and wrote a tanka about her.

STETHOSCOPE

I recoiled from the stethoscope
As if its touch
Were about to rob me of my thoughts.

The fear of objects—with the tube of the stethoscope like a snake—is evident here at a time when Takuboku is definitely not at all well.

COMING TO

Affection for my wife and daughter
Visiting the hospital
Has brought me back to myself.

The phrase in the original, *ware ni kaeri*, has an exact equivalent in "come back to oneself." This suggests that Takuboku is keenly aware that when feeling depressed he is not his real self. He is able to reaffirm his love for his wife and daughter; and this transports him, if temporarily, back to reality.

IN DESOLATION

Closing my eyes conjures nothing.
I've nothing to do
But open them again.

Usually closing the eyes allows an artist to contemplate some thought or image that may be useful in their work. Here he sees nothing, and this disturbs him.

ALL IN ONE NIGHT

What sort of grave mound is this dune
Built by the storm
That passed through the night?

A metaphor of death, involving nature as its architect. This grave may be a mound like the ones built in ancient Japan.

A VOID

I am furious with myself for this death wish
But cannot speak for the black void
In my heart.

The last word of this tanka, *munashisa* (futility, emptiness), makes its message bleak indeed, especially as it is modified by "black." He expresses a helplessness that makes it one of his darkest tanka. He is turning on himself and blaming himself.

ESCAPE

The sick beast of complaint
Has escaped my mind
For today.

Takuboku repeats *nigesareri* (escape, run away), setting the theme of this tanka. The respite given him seems to be short lived, due to the emphatic use of *kyo wa* (today).

THE COMING DAY OFF

Three years pass and every year
The same wish: to not get up
Till the next day.

Is this a kind of wish to be ill … or is it a wish to rest, to have time to think? Work must be hard, and the worker desires to do nothing for a day. But there are duties at home to perform, and even one day of vacation may be a luxury he cannot afford.

RAINING

The clanging pitter-patter of raindrops
Echoes in my aching head
Ringing despair.

The use of *tantaratara tantaratara* (loud pitter-patter, loud pitter-patter) is the kind of mimesis we associate more with Kenji than with Takuboku. I've repeated "-ing" four times to reinforce the effect of the rain on his mind.

ILL FOR SO LONG

I've been ill for so long
It delights me when I somehow forget
To take my medicine.

Takuboku has been ill for so long he can afford some irony. Illness has become the new normal for him.

OPERATION SCAR

Deep down I wish
For a new body
As I stroke my scar.

This tanka resembles the previous one in its somewhat bitter, yet droll, tone. The use of the verb *naderu* (to stroke, pet, caress) indicates that he feels tenderly toward this mark on his body.

MY THOUGHTS AGAIN

The pain in my chest today is intense.
If I am to die let me go and die
In my old hometown.

This is another often-quoted Takuboku tanka relating to his hometown in Iwate. He actually died in Tokyo. Again, he is writing about intentions that he is unable, for circumstances that may be either beyond or within his control, to bring into action.

FOUR MONTHS SICK IN BED

I cherish the memories
Of my medicines changing taste
With time.

This tanka and the succeeding one have the same first line, which I have used for the titles. In this one, Takuboku is gauging time in bed by the changing taste of his medicine. He describes his feelings toward this with a form of the word *natsukashii*, which indicates that it brings back fond memories.

FOUR MONTHS SICK IN BED

It touched me to the quick
To see how tall my daughter had grown
In such a short span of time.

In this tanka, too, Takuboku is expressing how the human mind strives to come to terms with the passage of time. If he cherished something in this span of time in the previous tanka, in this one he is reminded of how much he has lost in terms of contact with his family at the same time.

THE RAIN

When did summer come upon us
With the comfort for faint eyes
Of radiant rain?

Usually the brightness of a summer rain hurts the eyes, especially eyes that have become accustomed to the dark, as when one is in hospital for a long time. The brightness is comforting to him. After all, he has lived to see another summer.

SLEEPLESS NIGHTS

With my eyes flashing
From under the icepack
How I hated everyone on this Earth.

This tanka and the succeeding seven all describe what it is like to be ill or in the hospital: the loneliness and despair; the outlook on the outside as time passes; the encounters with the doctor; the weakness ... not even being strong enough to lift a book; the hopes ... about someday publishing a book; the chopsticks that are too heavy, despite the lightness of the salad. Even the apple is out of reach....

FEVER

My feverish eyes look sorrowfully
On the disarray of snow
Falling in spring.

THE ROUNDS

I rest my palms on my aching chest
And clamp my eyes shut.
Why is the doctor so slow in coming?

TODAY

The pain in my chest is more intense.
I've nothing to seek
Save a glimmer in my doctor's eyes.

IN BED

The weight alone of this book
Exhausts me, sending my mind
In all directions.

IN THE HOSPITAL

I rattled on to my wife
About the book I would definitely publish someday
Down to its cover and binding.

ILLNESS

I am entranced by the fresh colors
Of this salad. But it's all I can do
To lift the chopsticks.

TODAY

Racked by thirst I reach for an apple
But find my reach
Falling short.

TREMBLING

I feel so sorry for the young nurse
Dressed down by the doctor
Because her hand trembled on my pulse.

This tanka is about compassion and silent affection felt for a nurse dressed down by a doctor. The trembling of the nurse's hand on his pulse can be attributed to her trepidation at the hands of the angry doctor. Or is there another reason why she trembles when touching him?

PASSAGEWAY

Just once I'd love
To get to the far edge
Of that long hospital passageway.

That hospital corridor must seem so long to him. It is another way of describing his slow walk. It is as if he is thinking that he might be able to escape at the end of a passageway.

AUTUMN ON ITS WAY

Autumn is just over my shoulder.
How warm and intimate the skin on my fingers feels
Touching a light bulb.

It is soon to be autumn. His hands must be cold, though it is still technically summer. Can he get no warmth or intimacy from anything or anyone else save from a light bulb, which, by the way, would have been something quite new and exciting at the time?

BREATHING

The sound of breath leaving my lungs
Is lonelier
Than a biting winter's blast of wind.

He must be having trouble breathing. The sound is an omen.

DOCTOR

So now the doctor says to me
"We're going off to sleep now, aren't we?"
Speaking to me as if to a child.

The doctor's words, *nete irasshai*, are spoken in a manner that is used, for instance, by an adult to a child. That's why I chose to use "we" in the translation.

ADMIRING THE BEAUTY OF TULIPS

I dragged myself out of bed
But then wished for sleep again
After gazing upon those tulips with weary eyes.

Another tanka about weakness in illness and how it makes those rare moments when we can see beauty outside all the more precious.

PART FIVE

The Illusions of Self

Miyazawa Kenji used the term "mental sketch modified" to describe the poems he wrote. He saw them as temporary outpourings of his thoughts and feelings, modified by the chemistry of ink on paper. He insisted to the publisher of his only poetry book to come out in his lifetime that it was not to be called a collection of poems.

In a sense, Takuboku, too, writes "mental sketches" modified by the confines of the genre. But there seems to me to be a difference in approach between the two great poets of Iwate.

Kenji, for all his compassion for others, views the outside world through the prism of his own mental state. His descriptions of nature are not nature itself but the re-creation of nature in his mind. In one poem he refers to "the landscape of the heart." Kenji's eye on the world and himself is subjective in its essence.

Takuboku's eye on the world and himself is, on the other hand, essentially objective. Of course, he is the subject who observes, so he cannot disassociate himself entirely from what he sees outside himself. No one can do that. He is also the kind of portraitist who very often creates self-portraits. But he strives to be objective, to tell the "truth" about the world of others, as well as his own inner world.

For both poets the poetic self is an illusion. But it is an illusion that is invented and reinvented time and time again with each discrete observation and experience. When all of these discrete illusions are put together, we get a whole picture of the poet and his times.

Takuboku confesses that he is not always truthful to others and himself. Such confessions may not give him much comfort, but they provide comfort to us when we read the revelations because, thanks to his frankness, they allow us to be more open and honest about ourselves, to question our own opinions and feelings. This is the value of Takuboku's poetic objectivity.

Can we be sure, however, even with all of the insights into human nature that we have gained over the more than a century since Takuboku's death, that we know ourselves and represent ourselves more candidly to others than he did? I don't think so. We continue to hide our inner feelings, to fool ourselves into thinking we are kind and considerate, to prop up our self-important selves at the expense of others, as if we were little dolls in fancy dress perched on rising platforms.

Both Takuboku and Kenji are moralists in the sense that they teach us, in two very different ways, how to treat others with compassion and love.

If the self is an illusion, then it is one which we can fashion ourselves into something beautiful and, perhaps, dare I say, virtuous. These two poets of Iwate have a lot to teach us about the beauty and goodness of everyday life.

And it is virtue above all things that Ishikawa Takuboku and Miyazawa Kenji teach us: the virtue of creating a self that is a source of esteem to ourselves and worthy of the admiration of others.

And yet, he wrote ... Even considering all I have done / Up to now as a sham / Gives me no comfort.

PATHETIC SAND

How smoothly and easily this lifeless sand
Slips between the fingers
Of a fist!

Pathos, from the Greek word for suffering, is a quality that evokes both sadness and pity. Could it be that Takuboku is feeling that his own life is pathetic and "lifeless"? Though he makes a fist (the original uses the verb *nigiru*, to grasp), the sand slips through his fingers as if they were an hour glass. The adverb describing the way the sand falls is *sarasarato*, a mimetic word that indicates a soft, smooth and uninterrupted flow.

AUTUMN SCREAM

Having wandered into these fields
I scream out, recording my life
Dyed in verses of blood.

Takuboku wrote this tanka when his truant days at school were increasing; his place in class had sunk to number eighty-two out of 119; and he was caught cheating on a final mathematics exam in July 1902. In October he dropped out of school "for family reasons" and left Morioka for Tokyo. Hence the figurative blood....

THESE DAYS

I am considering prancing right up
To my biggest enemy.
I fold my arms on my chest.

Takuboku is "considering" doing it, but obviously doesn't. Inaction plagues him, even though he often gets very hot under the collar over some social evil or encounter. In this sense, he is very much like a lot of us: good intentions; no action.

SYCOPHANCY

I lose the plot
When I encounter sycophancy in others.
Sadly, I know myself only too well.

Quite a few of Takuboku's tanka refer at once to others and to himself. He exhibits a kind of self-deprecation that was not uncommon among intellectuals in the Meiji era. Later, when Japan expanded into China and the government demanded allegiance, people were either not allowed to or didn't have the strength to display self-deprecation. For *haratatsu*, I have chosen to use "lost the plot" instead of the more usual translation of "get angry." This is because I feel it better describes what happens to Takuboku and because the word "plot" has other meanings that are associated with him, such as the plot of a story and one to take some action or other.

PAST FUN

I used to knock on strangers' doors
Then make a quick escape.
I do wish I could go back!

Past fun can indicate fun from the past or fun that has passed and gone away. With "I do wish I could go back!" we don't know if he desires to relive the past in a nostalgic way or go back and make amends to the people whose doors he knocked on. In today's Japanese this is called *pin-nige*, literally "ding run away." The *pin* indicates the sound of a bell ringing, in this case a door bell. We also did this as kids and called it "ding dong dash," though I never considered going back.

SPONGE

I feel like a sponge soaked in water
Light by nature, yet
In reality, heavy.

This tanka, about the contradictory nature of Takuboku's mental and emotional state, begins with the mimetic word *shittori*. "Soak" is also a mimetic word in English, related in origin to suck, suckle, suction and succulent, all of which mimic a sound that water makes when it is moving in a particular way. The Japanese (and Chinese) word for "sponge" is written with the characters for "sea" and "cotton," visually reinforcing an image of absorption. The English word "sponge," coming all the way to us from Greek, Latin and Old Saxon, and similar to the word in many European languages, certainly has a mimetic quality in its combination of liquid letters.

ONE MORNING

The smell of simmering miso
Entered my nostrils just before awakening
From a sad dream.

The first line of this wonderful tanka contains Japanese alliteration that conjures up an image of the smell wafting through the air. Now that miso is enjoyed by people in many countries we can leave the word as it is, whereas some years ago it would be put in italics as a foreign word. It used to be the case that we translated miso with "bean paste." I don't know what I would do if I had to translate this line with "the smell of simmering bean paste." Thank goodness we've taken it into our kitchens.

FOR SOME REASON

There is a cliff inside my head.
And day by day, a fragment of earth
Crumbles off it.

This tanka's metaphor, of a slowly crumbling cliff, is visually stunning. It shows that Takuboku was very modern when it came to describing the symptoms of what we today generally call "depression."

IMPATIENCE

My impatience is like the impatience
Of hands that will not stop clapping
Until a sleepy voice responds.

This describes a rather abrupt and cruel way to awaken someone. Another possible translation for the word representing "impatience" is "irritation." Takuboku has the ease of skill to repeat even long words like *modokashisa* (impatience, irritation) in one line, taking up in Japanese ten syllables of the thirty-one-syllable length of the entire tanka. I sometimes think he is showing off when he does this, as if to say, "I can write whatever I want in only thirty-one syllables. No problem."

IT OCCURS TO ME

Anguish is a train
Coursing at times through my heart
As if crossing a wilderness.

Again, a metaphor that connects the inner world of his heart with the outer world of a train in the wilderness. The simple phrase "it occurs to me" emphasizes both an outer and an inner reality. The word he uses for "wilderness" can also mean "desert" and "wasteland."

FETAL POSITION

I bury myself in a fetal position
Under the futon cover and stick my tongue out
At no one in particular.

Takuboku, who so often wishes to return to childhood, willingly displays childish behavior here, but doesn't want anyone to see it ... except the reader.

TALKING BIG

A good half day talking big
To a guy even younger than me ...
How debilitating!

I first translated the last word, *tsukareshi-gokoro*, with "exhausting," but changed it to "debilitating" in a later draft. This word suggests that there may have been some harm to his body or psyche from this futile activity. This tanka resembles the succeeding one, in which he comes out openly about his selfish ego.

PRAISE

I cannot praise others
Unless I suppress my selfish ego.
It numbs me no end.

The key word in this tanka comes at the end: *sabishisa*. This can be translated in any number of ways, with "loneliness," "desolation," "sadness," and so on. I chose to emphasize the effect of loneliness on Takuboku by changing it from a noun into a verb. "It feeds my desolation" is another possible translation.

RECENT DAYS

Remorse plagues my silent heart.
It has drained the laughter
Right out of me.

This feeling of being drained by the experiences of life sometimes caused Takuboku to withdraw into himself; at other times it made him feel like running away from the routines of life. Here it is remorse that is defeating him.

I SEE IT NOW

I acted like an exceptional man.
Then I felt all empty inside.
There is no way to describe it.

The word he uses for "exceptional" is *hibon*. It can also be translated with "extraordinary," "unusual," "uncommon," and "prodigious." It is used to describe people with out-of-the-ordinary talent or exceptional genius.

IN ONE WAY OR ANOTHER

I picture myself
As a mass of lies
And just shut my eyes.

The three characters at the head of each Japanese line—"what," "self" and "eyes"— give this tanka a very strong impression of the self and how Takuboku sees it. The "what" is part of a phrase meaning "somehow" or "in one way or another," a phrase I transferred to the title. As I wrote in the Preface, by attaching titles to these tanka I have cheated in one way or another. It allows me to get information across that I would otherwise have had to squeeze into the three short lines. After all, the *tan* of tanka means "short."

PASSING THE MIRROR SHOP

They suddenly struck me
My seedy reflection …
My downtrodden gait.

This is a good example of what might be called "Takuboku Objectivity," his ability to view himself as if he were another person. This is at the core of his message to us as readers: Be honest with yourself, if with no one else. I decided to use "struck me" for *odorokinu* (which indicates surprise), because it conjures up an image of suddenness, as it underscores the reality of him stopping to look at himself in a shop window mirror on a walk about town.

TEARS

Tears seep into the sand
Forming beads.
How heavy those tears are!

Shittorito, which describes the manner in which the tears are being absorbed into the sand, is mimetic and suggestive of something that is dewy or wet. His tears seep into the sand, forming heavy beads. One of his two major collections of tanka is titled *A Handful of Sand*.

YOUNG GIRLS

Young girls would take my wailing
For that of a sick dog
Howling at the moon.

The English word "wail" is related to the word "woe," and it is mimetic. The word "howl" is also mimetic, related to the now rare word "ululate." You can almost hear Takuboku crying in vain in this tanka. It is no wonder that someone innocent would take him for a sick dog. Again, Takuboku is filled with self-deprecation, comparing himself unfavorably when seen through the eyes of others. His objectivity shines bitterly through this metaphor.

THE JAPANESE ISLE

Tears stream down my cheeks
Into the coarse white sand.
And I amuse myself with a crab.

Another very famous tanka by Takuboku, one studied in Japanese schools and one that speaks loudly of his loneliness and isolation. The word used to describe what he is doing with a crab is *tawamuru*, which can mean "play with," "amuse oneself" or even "flirt with," all of which just underscores his loneliness and his self-piteous fixation.

NATURE

I put the flower pot beside the brazier
To make its little plum blossom bloom overnight.
But it refused to flower.

Humans cannot make nature do what isn't natural. We can't always make other people act like we would like them to either. It is winter, and Takuboku is hoping to speed up the arrival of spring.

ACCIDENT

I accidently broke a teacup
Then relived the pleasant sensation
This morning.

Takuboku is often struck by mixed, almost paradoxical, feelings. Regret to him is both bitter and sweet. The breaking of a teacup does seem like an unfortunate accident, but he is nonetheless savoring the *kimochiyosa* (agreeable feeling, nice sensation) of what he did.

SOURCE OF SORROW

It is the autumn wind
That causes normally dry eyes to stream
Ceaselessly.

The last word in the original is *nagaruru*, a traditional form of the word "to flow" that has a lyrical and flowing quality of its own. Takuboku is not feeling, to quote a phrase from Kenji, "strong in the wind."

IN SPITE OF MYSELF

I couldn't laugh in spite of myself.
The knife I looked everywhere for
Was in my hand all the time.

Self-irony or, if taken literally, self-hatred? We have all looked for things that we are actually carrying, but when it's a knife....

IS THIS THE MAN

Is this the man I have become
Not looking up at the sky once
In the span of four or five years?

Takuboku is asking himself if he has lost his ideals while concentrating too long on mundane matters. The meaning of the first line, which is in the third line of the original, can also be interpreted, "Is this what becomes of a person?"

NIGHT MATCH

Strike a match
And a white moth will appear
To cross through two feet of air.

Takuboku has created a metaphor here. Like the moth, we humans can only see things in the lit area that is close to us. Our world is defined by the light we can see or create for ourselves, and no more. The moth, in fact, will probably fly right back into the dark, where it will be unseen by us. Or … will its attraction to the light be its end?

JUST NOW

A cuckoo cried out in my dream.
It causes me grief that this cuckoo
Will not let me be.

A literal translation of *wasurezari* is "cannot forget" or "cannot get out of the mind." I have interpreted this to mean that he is preoccupied at this moment with the cry of the cuckoo and it won't let him alone. Of course, the phrase "will not let me be" also means "will not let me exist." These sounds from the past, be they from nature or people, continued to haunt him until the day he died.

THIS MORNING

That's it, I've made up my mind.
"No more lying" …
Except for the one I just told.

When he makes this vow to himself in the new morning, at least he sees its hypocrisy in a humorous light.

FABRICATIONS

Everything up to now has been a fabrication.
But even this confession to myself
Gives me no consolation.

Like the preceding tanka, this one deals with fabrication and confession, though it doesn't make him feel a bit better about himself. There is an alternate translation of this tanka in the introduction to this chapter.

DYED

I am uneasy, insecure
Able solely to stare at my nails
Dyed by the juice of mandarin oranges.

Japanese people used to eat mandarin oranges in a different way than they do now. I saw this when I arrived in Japan in 1967. A bowl of them would be sitting in the middle of the table, as everyone in the family peeled one and then carefully picked the pith off it before sucking out the flesh and discarding the little membrane around it. Over time this would certainly leave a little stain on the nails. The passage of time is evident in this tanka. One can see Takuboku sitting for hours at a table eating mandarin oranges, wishing he was able to pick up a pen.

FOR NEARLY HALF A DAY

I picked at the hard bark on the tall tree
With my fingertips.
My ear was flush against the trunk.

The contrast between hard bark of the tree and soft skin of the fingers and ear, as well as the contrast in scale between the tall tree and a small ear, is striking. Is this a metaphor for the frustrations of life? Is Takuboku trying to get a message from nature? If so, it seems futile here.

INTERLUDE

It pleases me no end to hear
The clock sounding the hour
In this rare peaceful interlude.

Omoshiroku kiku (to hear or listen to with interest or pleasure) refers here to the pleasure he gets from life's little discoveries. Is he unable to sleep in the middle of the night? Or is he alone, not "bothered" by family?

DRIFTWOOD

I look around before addressing
The driftwood left at the edge
Of a sand dune.

Like wood that drifts, Takuboku sees himself as an object that is taken from one place to another by circumstances. He finds himself with no one to talk to and seems so embarrassed to be speaking to a piece of wood that he looks around to make sure he is alone.

SOMETHING IS TELLING ME

Something is telling me
To bolt across this meadow
Until there is no breath left in me.

The first line is *naniganashini* in Japanese. This can mean "for no particular reason" or, simply, "somehow." But there is something prompting Takuboku to take this impulsive action. The trouble is that he doesn't know what it is himself.

THE SELF

I was a man who sadly thought
The world revolved around him.
I can't get over the thought.

Takuboku is sometimes repulsed by his egotism, yet somehow unable to free himself from it. The "self against the self" is a major theme in his tanka, and it is a theme we see taken up by many writers around the world in the twentieth century. Takuboku is a pioneer of modernism.

WHAT IT'S LIKE

It's like a tired cow's drool
A thin trickle, always the same
And, it seems, endless.

The cow's drool is an old metaphor in Japan for tireless endurance, for something that is persistent. It is used in the proverb *Akinai wa ushi no yodare*, or "Business is like the cow's drool." This means that the pursuit of profit should be conducted in a "long, thin and unbroken" way, not rushed through or blasted out. But I don't think Takuboku is talking about business here. Even though he leaves the subject out, and the "it" can stand for anything, I assume he means life in general. "Trickle" is a mimetic equivalent of the Japanese in the tanka, *taratarato*.

THESE DAYS

Remorse has stealthily lodged in my heart.
It has drained the laughter
Out of me.

Takuboku sometimes uses the word *hisokani* (secretly, stealthily) to describe an occurrence in his heart that comes upon him subconsciously. The use of the verb *yadoru*, "to dwell, lodge or take shelter in," seems to indicate that although he writes that this has happened "these days," the remorse may have been with him for a long time and may remain within him. This is a tanka that well describes what it is like to have depression.

WHAT IS IT?

What is it that has freed my mind
As I roll this little crystal ball
Over the lines of my palm?

This tanka is about how Takuboku views his future, that is, with uncertainty. And yet, this uncertainty is liberating rather than frightening. He just doesn't understand the mechanism. He published this tanka on 18 June 1910 in the Asahi Shimbun, then called the Tokyo Asahi Shimbun. But in an earlier version he explicitly says that he receives joy when he rolls the ball in his hand. In this final version, however, it is clear that he can't put his finger on why this little action makes him feel liberated. This is a good example of how leaving something out adds to the mystery and power of the polished poem.

A DOG BY THE SIDE OF THE ROAD

A dog yawned a big yawn
And I yawned too, copying it
Full of envy.

Takuboku obviously feels not only envious of the dog but also affectionate toward it.
Is the dog bored like he is, or merely tired out?

IN THE MORNING SOME FOUR DAYS AGO

I awoke to find
That I had been arguing with God and weeping.
What a dream that was!

Some people seem to interpret this dream as a kind of nightmare. After all, when
we are ill, as Takuboku was, we tend to have bad dreams. In addition, he wept. But
I think that Takuboku sees this as a good dream. After all, he got the chance to
argue with God. Perhaps he is thankful that he is still well enough that he can weep
over issues he might be discussing with God. The Japanese *ano yume yo!* ("What
a dream!" or "Oh, that dream!") doesn't give us a clue as to whether it was a good
dream or not.

NEIGHBORHOOD CHILDREN

I can't figure the neighborhood children out.
I wanted to play with them today and called to them.
Not a single one came.

Well, he's not exactly one of them. And besides, as he well knows, children don't like to be around glum and grumpy adults.

MY SKIN

The city sleeps.
And I sense heavy footsteps
Through every pore of my body.

There is something ominous about this tanka. The "heavy footsteps" that seem to be penetrating his skin may be emanating from his own heart.

I TELL MYSELF

I sometimes tell myself
"You're pathetic, Ishikawa!"
It really gets me down.

He is so self-deprecating here as to be self-destructive. "It really gets me down" is another way to translate a form of the word that crops up so often in Takuboku's tanka, *kanashii*, "sad."

FATE

I woke up in the dead of night
With the heavy futon cover over me.
Is fate bearing down on me?

Takuboku certainly felt the weight of the world bearing down on him. He cared so much for humanity that his cares became a burden to him. Was this his fate, or could he have thrown off the heavy futon cover and changed his life?

TEARS

A flood of tears … how bizarre!
They flow
And I am awash in giddiness.

One of the symptoms of bipolar disorder is sudden and extreme mood swings. Takuboku's personality, at least as expressed in his tanka, certainly displays these signs. They are also evident in the personality of his soul mate from Iwate, Miyazawa Kenji. They had more in common than just being from the same prefecture and having attended the same school.

A HANDFUL OF SAND

He does not wipe his cheeks clean of tears
The man who produced a handful of sand.
Not to be forgotten …

What is it that is not to be forgotten, that he will not wipe his cheeks of tears, or that he is the man who wrote a book called *A Handful of Sand*. It is both.

WEB

I left the woods without seeing you
And found myself caught up in the web
Of a spider larger than a leopard.

In the end, despite all their realism and soul searching, some of his most startling images are imaginary and larger than life. Are life and poetry real or just an illusion? This is one crucial question at the core of the poetry of Ishikawa Takuboku. It can be seen starkly and poignantly in the last tanka of this collection, "White Dog."

WHITE DOG

I turn to my wife
And ask if I can keep a white dog
Like the one I see outside the garden.

Afterword

Ishikawa Takuboku was born in Iwate prefecture on 20 February 1886 in a little village not far from Shibutami, where his family moved when he was one year old. Takuboku is a pen name; his given name was Hajime. His father was chief priest at a Buddhist temple. He attended primary school at Shibutami, and the school, with the very same classroom in which he sat, is beautifully preserved today alongside the museum dedicated to his life and work. He moved on to middle school in the prefectural capital, Morioka, where he first met and became infatuated with Horiai Setsuko. By age sixteen he was producing work of such quality that his tanka were accepted by the premier tanka (and later literary and arts) journal, "Myojo," and he promptly dropped out of school to pursue a career in literature.

It wasn't long before he was recognized by the likes of Yosano Tekkan and his wife Akiko, the leading lights in the genre of tanka, as a brilliant new voice. At the beginning of May 1905 he published his first collection of poetry, "Akogare" ("Yearning") and, at the end of the month, married Setsuko. The little home in Morioka that they moved into still stands and can be visited today. Takuboku, who was in Sendai scrounging loans from friends, missed his own wedding, obliging his bride to wait at the home for him until 4 June. Since his parents and younger sister, Mitsuko, were also living at the house, the family discord that is a major theme of his poetry was to rear its head quite early on in the marriage.

Setsuko gave birth to a daughter, Kyoko, at the end of December 1906. Adding to the domestic turbulence was the defrocking of his father for failing to pay dues, leaving Takuboku as the family's breadwinner.

"Akogare," a collection of seventy-seven poems, is the kind of lyrical outpouring one would expect from a disaffected, sentimental and self-indulgent young man. He would not come into his own as the keenest observer of his life and times until 1910 and 1912, when his two major collections of tanka, "Ichiaku no Suna" (*A Handful of Sand*) and "Kanashiki Gangu" (*Sad Toys*), came out. *Sad Toys* was published in June 1912, two months after his death.

In 1907, Takuboku traveled alone to Hakodate in Hokkaido, becoming a substitute teacher at a primary school. However, the school burned down in a fire and he went to Sapporo, where, in August, he found work as a proofreader at a newspaper. By September he was in Otaru, this time writing for a daily, the Otaru Nippo. A violent altercation with an editor in December brought an abrupt end to that employment.

Takuboku moved to Tokyo in 1908, and the next year began work again as a proofreader, now at the Tokyo Asahi Shimbun, today's Asahi Shimbun. His wife, daughter and mother joined him there, but the atmosphere in the home was, at best, strained and, at worst, internecine. A son, Shinichi, was born to the couple in 1910, but the infant died three weeks after birth.

Takuboku himself was plagued by illness but could ill afford to see a doctor. He was urgently hospitalized in 1911 and diagnosed with chronic peritonitis, spending forty days in hospital after surgery. His mother died of tuberculosis in March 1912; and on 13 April, he passed away from the same illness, age twenty-six.

After his death, Setsuko took Kyoko to Awa in Chiba Prefecture, where she gave birth to another daughter, Fusae. In September of that year, she returned to her family home in Hakodate with the two girls. In March 1913, Takuboku's ashes were brought to Hakodate and interred there. Setsuko died of tuberculosis in May of that year, age twenty-eight. The daughters succumbed to illness in December 1930: Kyoko to pneumonia at age twenty-three, and Fusae to tuberculosis at eighteen, both dying at a younger age than their parents were when they passed away.

Takuboku had begun writing diaries in 1902, the most famous of them being his "Romaji Nikki" (*Diary in Roman Letters*), which he wrote in that script, for one reason, as an obstacle to his wife's reading it. In fact, his tanka taken together also form a kind of diary of events, internal and external. Takuboku wrote that poetry itself was a report in detail of changes in an individual's emotions. His diaries and his poetry are permeated with a sincere and searching self-examination. They are deep stabs at truth.

He fell hopelessly in love with a number of women, the most acclaimed in his poetry being Tachibana Chieko and the geisha Koyakko, whose real name was Konoe Jin. Tachibana, a fellow teacher in Hakodate, did not return his affection and married someone else. Takuboku was, after all, a married man. The truly beautiful Koyakko, however, had ardent feelings for him. She possessed an incisive intellect and recognized his talent. She also possessed the most famous earlobes in Japanese literary history (see page forty). Koyakko died in 1965, outliving her poet lover by fifty-three years.

Takuboku is a model of hope and inspiration for today's self-sequestered people, with his ardent commitment to life and word, his constant seeking of something better for himself, his family, to whom he was devoted in his own way, and his care for people who found themselves living in the lower economic and social strata in his country.

He is a model to all, not only for this candor and compassion, but for his insight into his own psyche and his willingness to share it unequivocally. There is nothing devious or calculating about

Takuboku. If such a tendency does show up, he is the first to put his finger on it and bathe it in a bright light.

In the mirror of his works we are compelled to examine the features of our own face in this bright and wholly revealing light as it reaches us, without diminishing in magnitude, from another time.